T0277312

WHAT
REMAINS

WHAT REMAINS

THE COLLECTED POEMS OF
HANNAH ARENDT

Translated and edited by

SAMANTHA ROSE HILL WITH GENESE GRILL

Liveright Publishing Corporation

An Imprint of W. W. Norton & Company
Independent Publishers Since 1923

For Jerome Kohn

For information about permission to reproduce selections from this book, write to
Permissions, Liveright Publishing Corporation, a division of W. W. Norton & Company, Inc.,
500 Fifth Avenue, New York, NY 10110

For information about special discounts for bulk purchases, please contact
W. W. Norton Special Sales at specialsales@wwnorton.com or 800-233-4830

Manufacturing by Lakeside Book Company
Book design by Chris Welch
Production manager: Louise Mattarelliano

ISBN 978-1-324-09052-6

Liveright Publishing Corporation
500 Fifth Avenue, New York, N.Y. 10110
www.wwnorton.com

W. W. Norton & Company Ltd.
15 Carlisle Street, London W1D 3BS

10 9 8 7 6 5 4 3 2 1

Contents

PART I

1923–1926

Winter 1923–1924

PART II
1942–1961

1942

1943

1959

1960

1961

Introduction

The Mother Tongue

In the spring of 1975 Hannah Arendt flew to Denmark to accept the Sonning Prize from the Danish government in recognition of her "contributions to European civilization." She began her acceptance speech with an uncharacteristic moment of self-reflection:

> I am, as you know, a Jew, *feminini generis* as you can see, born and educated in Germany as, no doubt, you can hear, and formed to a certain extent by eight long and rather happy years in France. . . . if I ever did anything consciously for European civilization, it certainly was nothing but the deliberate intent, from the moment I fled Germany, not to exchange my mother tongue against whatever language I was offered or forced to use.[1]

Arendt reminded the audience that such honors are usually bestowed after one has died, and her otherwise forceful voice took on an air of vulnerability. She was the first American and first woman to win the prize, but these facts did not matter to her. It was the acknowledgment of her life's work, born in exile from Germany, that unsettled the carefully separated veil she had drawn between her private and public life. As a young philosophy student, more comfortable in the library than doing politics in the street, she never intended to live her life publicly. She liked her solitude and guarded it. Even amid the international fallout after the publication of *Eichmann in Jerusalem,* and her subsequent banishment from Jewish and New York society, Arendt kept her emotional distance, separating the personal from the political. But in this moment of recognition, she dropped the mask, though not without first reflecting—in more characteristic form—on the etymological root of the word "mask," and what it means to appear in public and speak before others: "Persona, at any event, originally referred to the actor's mask that covered his individual 'personal' face and indicated to the spectator the role and the part of the actor in the play."[2]

Until Hannah Arendt's archives were opened by the American novelist Mary McCarthy in 1988, her poems remained part of her private life. It is unknown whether she ever tried to publish them. (It seems doubtful, as they would have revealed too much.) It is also unknown whether she shared them with Robert Lowell, W. H. Auden, Hermann Broch, or Randall Jarrell, who often consulted her about their own work. (It seems possible, as they often conversed in private over bottles of wine.) From dedications and acknowledgments we know that she lent a verse or two from time to time: "Thanks for several lines," Lowell writes to her in a dedication to one of his books.[3] But as Elisabeth Young-Bruehl wrote in her biography *Hannah Arendt: For Love of the World,* "[V]ery few people—including her first husband—knew that she wrote poetry. Her poems were her most private life."[4] I'd edit Young-Bruehl's assessment: Her poems were her private life.

—

Arendt wrote poems to record events, reflect on experiences, and engage in what she called "the free play of thinking." From the time she began collecting her poems in the winter of 1923, they remained among her most prized possessions. When she fled Germany in the spring of 1933, after being released from the Gestapo prison at Alexanderplatz in Berlin, she put the twenty-one poems she had written into a suitcase containing her birth certificate, passport, marriage documents, doctoral diploma, correspondence, and manuscripts. She carried them with her over the Ore Mountains to Prague, then to Geneva, where she spent a few months as a recording secretary for the League of Nations. She took them to Paris, where she lived in the Hôtel Soufflot, and they remained with her as she divorced her first husband, then met, fell in love with, and married her second husband, Heinrich Blücher. She held on to them for eight years in exile as she worked with Youth Aliyah to help Jewish youth escape to Palestine. She carried them with her when she was forced to report for transit to the Gurs internment camp—with instructions to carry one suitcase under thirty kilograms—in the spring of 1940. And they went with her when she escaped five weeks later, walking out of the camp alone with forged papers as the German front approached. She held on to them as she walked across France to Lourdes, and then to Montauban, in the hope of reuniting with her husband. She took them as they rode bicycles to Marseilles looking for emergency exit papers; on the train to Portbou to find Walter Benjamin's grave; and to Lisbon, where she waited for several months to board the SS *Guinee*. And she carried them with her as she crossed the Atlantic Ocean to New York City.

When Arendt arrived at Ellis Island on May 22, 1941, she was thirty-four years old and did not speak English, save, she claimed, a few lines of William Shakespeare. She spent her first summer as a housekeeper in Winchester, Massachusetts, learning the language through conversation and a collection of books her host left on her nightstand, including an English-German dictionary.[5] When she returned to New York in the fall, she began her writing career in America with the help of Salo Baron, a Jewish historian at Columbia University who oversaw the journal *Social Studies*. Her first essays on Franz Kafka, Heinrich Heine, and Bernard Lazare were written in German and translated into English. Over the next ten years Arendt worked as a journalist, lecturer, research director for the Conference on Jewish Relations, chief editor for Schocken Books, and executive director for the Jewish Cultural Reconstruction, Inc., under whose auspices she helped recover 1.5 million Jewish artifacts that had been stolen by the Nazis. She edited Kafka's diaries for publication, brought Gershom Scholem's work on Jewish mysticism to America, and took meetings with T. S. Eliot. She published her first major work, *The Origins of Totalitarianism*, in 1951, the same year she was granted American citizenship and legally changed her name from Johanna to Hannah. During this first decade in New York, as she made a home on the Upper West Side, Arendt typed up the twenty-one poems she had written before being forced into exile and added them to the ones she wrote between 1942 and 1950. She edited and self-bound the poems into two small volumes, which are now housed in Arendt's archive at the Library of Congress in Washington, D. C., in Container 79, Folder: Miscel-

lany: Poems and Stories, 1925–1942 and Undated, which is where
I found them.

—

To introduce Hannah Arendt as a poet to English-speaking read-
ers is to introduce Hannah Arendt as a thinker who remained
deeply rooted in the German language. On January 1, 1933, as
Germany catapulted toward totalitarianism, Arendt wrote to her
mentor and friend, the existentialist philosopher Karl Jaspers,
"For me, Germany means my mother tongue, philosophy, and lit-
erature."[6] It was not the country she identified with, but the lan-
guage. And for Arendt, this included the poems she memorized
in her youth. It was the language of the great German poets—
Goethe, Hölderlin, Schiller, and Rilke—that she carried around
in her *Hinterkopf,* the back of her mind.

When her first essays in America were translated from German
to English, Arendt was sensitive to the language—what was lost,
what was gained—making lists of substitutions for her editors.
Instead of resignation, compromise. Instead of despair, failure.
Instead of cognition, dependence. Instead of inability of perfec-
tion, accept it. Instead of would, must. Instead of supposed reality,
fiction. Instead of two human beings, two men. During a panel
discussion at the University of Toronto in 1972, Arendt recounted
a story from her early publishing days in New York:

> When I came to this country I wrote in my very halting
> English a Kafka article, and they had it "Englished" for the
> *Partisan Review.* And when I came to talk to them about the
> Englishing I read the article and there of all things the word
> "progress" appeared. I said: "What do you mean by this, I

never used that word," and so on. And then one of the editors went to the other in another room, and left me there, and I overheard him say, in a tone of despair, "she doesn't even believe in progress."[7]

But ultimately it was the New York poets who taught Arendt how to "English" her writing, and who introduced her to the world of English poetry.

Living in exile, Arendt found a home in her husband, whom she called her "four walls"; her inner circle of friends, whom she called her "tribe"; and her mother tongue, which she retained. Her apartments at 317 West 95th Street and later 370 Riverside Drive were refuges overflowing with wine and liquor. The cigarette smoke and laughter conferred an opulence to an otherwise unfashionable green sofa worn threadbare from hours of conversation over Campari and Chesterfields.[8] "West Side intellectuals with European backgrounds gather in one room, and West Side intellectuals with American backgrounds gather in another. The Europeans are in the room with the liqueurs and chocolates. The Americans are in the room with the whisky," wrote a *New York Times* reporter who attended one of Arendt's famous parties.[9]

Arendt formed relationships with the Austrian writer and poet Hermann Broch, as well as the poet Robert Lowell, and a close friendship with W. H. Auden, who after her husband's death proposed they platonically marry to take care of one another in old age. She drank with Robert Gilbert; crossed paths with Edward Albee, Langston Hughes, and e.e. cummings; and even entertained Elizabeth Bishop on occasion. "Dear Hannah Arendt: You may not remember me, but I spent two evenings at your apartment long ago," Bishop once wrote. Arendt responded, "Dear

Elizabeth Bishop, What an idea that I won't remember you. I remember every minute of that remarkable evening with your Brazilian friend and to tell the truth I was always disappointed that I never heard from you again . . ."[10] She spent long evenings in her apartment with the critic Randall Jarrell and described their time together as a kind of seduction:

> He read English poetry to me for hours, old and new, only rarely his own, which, however, for a time, he used to mail as soon as the poems came out of the typewriter. He opened up for me a whole new world of sound and meter, and he taught me the specific gravity of English words, whose relative weight, in all languages, is ultimately determined by poetic usage and standards.[11]

She shared Goethe, Schiller, and Rilke with him, and in turn he introduced her to Emily Dickinson, William Wordsworth, and Auden. Lowell described Arendt in those years as an "oasis in the fevered, dialectical dust of New York."[12] He first met Arendt in the late 1950s, in Mary McCarthy's apartment, through Jarrell, who had written to him about her work years earlier. Jarrell had told Lowell to read *The Origins of Totalitarianism* if he "wanted to discover something big and new." In Arendt's writing Lowell experienced a sense of homecoming. "I felt landless and alone," he wrote, "and read Hannah as though I were going home, or reading *Moby-Dick*, perhaps for the second time, no longer seeking adventure, but the voyage of wisdom, the tragedy of America."[13] Lowell dedicated the last poem in his collection *Imitations* to Arendt, adding a stanza he'd carried around since he was a boy about the Greek warrior Leonidas. He sent her a copy with a letter calling it his "finest poem."

Pigeons (for Hannah Arendt)
The same old flights, the same old homecomings,
dozens of each per day,
but at least the pigeon gets clear of the pigeon-house . . .
What is home, but the feeling of homesickness
for the flight's lost moment of fluttering terror?

W. H. Auden had a similar response when he read Arendt for the first time, sensing an affinity between their ways of thinking. In his 1959 review of *The Human Condition* for *Encounter* magazine, he wrote, "Every now and then, I come across a book which gives me the impression of having been especially written for me. In the case of a work of art, the author seems to have created a world for which I have been waiting all my life. . . ."[14] When Auden visited Arendt at 370 Riverside Drive, her neighbors often called the police on him because they thought he was a homeless man trying to break into the building. For years Arendt begged him to let her buy him another suit. "A man needs two," she'd tell him. But Auden refused and Arendt embraced his unkempt appearance, comparing his genius to that of Goethe and Pushkin. His ability to take the idioms of everyday language and transform them in their "utter simplicity" made his work untranslatable, which Arendt said was the mark of a great poem. Through language, Auden was able to make visible what otherwise remained hidden in the invisible realm of the mind.

—

After the burning of the Reichstag in February 1933, Arendt had turned away from the world of professional thinking. She said she wanted nothing more to do with that milieu of academic intellectuals, as she watched friends, lovers, and professors go along with the Nazification of Germany. For Arendt, the work of philosophy had blinded those around her to the horrors of reality by divorcing thinking from experience. And when the chips were down, it turned out, the professional thinkers were the least reliable thinkers of all. "Explain why intellectuals can be attracted by a totalitarian ideology," she asked students on an exam she gave in 1955, still grappling with the aftermath of the war. It was the professional thinkers, she observed, who so readily went along with the tide of tyrannical thinking. In one of her notebooks she asks: "Is there a way of thinking that is not tyrannical?" She never offers a direct response to this question, but my wager is that if she had, it would have been poetic thinking. All thinking moves from experience, she said, and poetry is the form closest to thinking itself.

It wasn't that Arendt wrote poems because she was a student of poetry who was taught to write poems, or because she fancied herself a secret poet, or because she felt the muse speaking through her. Though, who is to say. Arendt wrote poems because she had found in them a language that allowed her to weave together thinking and experience. In his remembrance of Arendt, the political scientist Hans Morgenthau reflected: "Her mind worked in a way not dissimilar to the poetic mind, which creates affinities, which discovers relationships that appear obvious once they are formulated but that nobody had thought of before the poet formulated them." The language of poetry was a way of thinking for Arendt; it was what she called, "poetic thinking."

And one need not write poems to be a poetic thinker. In *Men in Dark Times*, she reflects, "Hermann Broch was a poet in spite of himself." Remembering Jarrell, she wrote, "What I mean to say is that Randall Jarrell would have been a poet if he had never written a single poem." Similarly, for Walter Benjamin: "What is so hard to understand about Benjamin is that without being a poet he thought poetically." And in her essay on Bertolt Brecht, titled "What is Permitted to Jove," she reflects, "The first thing to be pointed out is that poets have not often made good, reliable citizens." She adds that Plato himself was a great poet, merely disguised as a philosopher.[15]

Many of Arendt's published works—from *The Human Condition* (1958), *Between Past and Future* (1961), *On Revolution* (1963), and *Men in Dark Times* (1968) to her final, unfinished work, *The Life of the Mind*, which Mary McCarthy edited and published in two volumes in 1977–78—draw upon the language of poems. In *The Human Condition* Arendt turns to Rilke to discuss how intense experiences of bodily pain are the least communicable human experiences, citing a poem he wrote on his deathbed. *Between Past and Future* begins with a quotation from the French poet and resistance fighter René Char, and the same quotation ends *On Revolution*: "Our inheritance was left to us by no testament." And in *The Life of the Mind* she turns to Auden and Shakespeare and the "timeless track that thinking beats into the world of space and time," to conceptualize where we are when we think, to address those old questions of meaning and being in philosophy. Instead of asking how or when, Auden's verse prompted her to ask: where? In these poets Arendt found a new vocabulary, rich in metaphor, that empowered her to think the world anew.

Arendt afforded poets a distinct place in the social hierarchy of the world, set apart from mere mortal judgment. "A poet's real sins are avenged by the gods of poetry," she wrote in an essay on Brecht. She describes how, at birth, the gods lean over the cradle and decide whether a child will be blessed with a poetic voice. "Poetry," she argued, "whose material is language, is perhaps the most human and least worldly of the arts, the one in which the end product remains closest to the thought that inspired it."[16] She did not side with Goethe, who thought poetry was form given to nature. Nor with the German philosopher Johann Gottfried Herder, who described poetry as a "magic force that affects" the soul. Nor even with Gotthold Ephraim Lessing, who said the essence of poetry is action. One might argue that she sided with Auden, who claimed "poetry makes nothing happen: it survives."[17]

But for Arendt the demand was much greater. It is the poets alone who bear the burden of truth in our world. They are our record-keepers, tending the storehouse of language and memory.

—

The seventy-one poems in this volume span thirty-eight years of Arendt's life and are presented in chronological order, keeping with Arendt's own method of organization. They can be roughly divided into two parts: the first contains twenty-one poems she wrote before she was forced to flee Germany, and the second contains poems she wrote in her notebooks and correspondence mostly after the war. The first section of Part One is dated "Winter 1923–1924." The first poem, written when Arendt was seventeen or eighteen years old, wrestles with the existence of God:

No word breaks the dark—
No god lifts a hand—
Wherever I look
This tremendous land.
No shadow hovers,
No form has weight.
And still I hear:
Too late, too late.

Several of the poems written between 1923 and 1926 were written for or about Martin Heidegger. Arendt kept her poems a secret during her lifetime, and so too her relationship with Heidegger. It wasn't until her archive was opened in the 1980s that their romance became public knowledge. Arendt met Heidegger in the fall of 1924 when she went to study with him at the University of Marburg. Students from across the country traveled to study with the "magician from Messkirch" who made Plato and Aristotle come to life when he spoke. After their first meeting in his office, Heidegger wrote to Arendt, telling her that he had to speak to her at once. He declared his love two weeks later. They met in his office, in the woods, in the meadows, in her tiny attic apartment where she kept a pet mouse. These early poems offer the reader a glimpse into their relationship—the desire, the longing, the frustration:

> Why do you give your hand to me
> Shy and like a secret?
> Do you come from such a faraway land,
> That you do not know our wine?

The inner world of her youth was a landscape colored by the language of romanticism, a sense of otherness, feelings of uselessness, difficulty with the vulnerability required of love, and uncertainty about God. Fields, trees, meadows, blossoming flowers, and a sense of ironic justice appear as she tries to understand her place in the world, as both a woman and a thinker:

> I myself,
> I'm dancing too.
> Ironically foolish,
> I've forgotten nothing,

I know the emptiness,
I know the burden,
I dance, I dance
In ironic splendor

Many of Arendt's poems read as records—records of youth, of love, of loss, of place and time. You won't find William Carlos Williams's cold plums in the fridge or Wallace Stevens's glass jars on hills. Arendt doesn't describe the material details of ordinary life; objects rarely appear in her poems symbolically, or otherwise. Instead she relies upon the language of atmosphere to capture feelings of longing, restlessness, melancholia, frustrated love, and death. Her language, never pointillist, is more like the stroke of a palette knife. Darkness, night, brown, yellow, green, blue, empty space, void, silence, a touch of air, a trace of a hand, an echo of a whisper, a passing train, the sound of prayer—these are the colors, sounds, and images that texture Arendt's poems. They belong to what she might have called factual truth, that is, what she experienced with her senses, recollected, remembered, and recorded in verse.

Arendt's poems often assume a conversational tone, as if sitting on a park bench with a friend watching passersby. In a poem from 1943 written shortly after her arrival in America, she describes Riverside Park near her apartment:

Fishers fish quietly on rivers
    In the world.
Drivers drive blindly on roads
    Around the world.

Many of Arendt's postwar poems reflect upon the losses of war—lost friends, lost landscapes, and a lost sense of certainty about the world. Some of these poems were written during her travels and enclosed in her correspondence with Blücher, like the lines from this poem written in 1946:

> I know that the streets are destroyed.
> Where are the wagon tracks, miraculously unscathed,
> shining forth from ancient ruins?

> I know that the houses have fallen.
> We entered the world in them, wonderfully sure, that they
> were more durable than ourselves.

Most of the poems written between 1950 and 1961 appear in notebooks marked "June 1950 to 1971." The twenty-eight, five-by-eight mottled brown Champion Line Wiremaster notebooks are housed in the German Literature Archive in Marbach, Germany. Arendt's notebooks provided a space where she could conduct what she called "thinking exercises," the term used by Albert Einstein to describe how he arrived at his General Theory of Relativity. Throughout, she can be seen editing her poems, crossing out lines, trying out new ones.[18] She used the page as one might use a stage, arranging voices to place herself in conversation with others. She copied out lines from Goethe, Hölderlin, Milton, Rilke, Pascal, Faulkner, Wordsworth, and Melville, as well as Latin phrases—*nemo ante mortem magnus; de nemine bene nisi de mortuis*—and even lyrics from folksongs, "One is one and all alone / And evermore shall be so." The first poem that appears in her collected notebooks reads:

Oh, who cares
What we are and how we appear.
It doesn't make a difference to them,
What we do or think.

The sky is in flames,
Heaven is on fire
Above us all,
Who don't know the way.

The final poem we have, which appears in a late notebook, is labeled "January 1961, Evanston." Arendt had agreed to teach two courses that winter—a lecture course, "On Revolution," and an upper-level seminar on the beginnings of political philosophy—during the winter quarter of 1961 at Northwestern University in Evanston, Illinois. She was to be in residence for three months that spring, but she rearranged her schedule to attend the trial of Adolf Eichmann in Jerusalem. At the end of January, Blücher was supposed to visit her in Evanston for his birthday, but he decided not to leave New York at the last minute and never arrived.

Then I will run as I ran before
Through grass and trees and fields;
Then you will stand as you once stood
The most heartfelt greeting in the world.

Then the steps will be counted
By what is near and what is far;
Then this life will be recounted
as a dream from long ago.

◆

Translating these poems has been a peregrination between German and English, as we've attempted to tend to the German roots while caring for the English appearance. The English writing style that Arendt developed in New York is marked by German syntax and grammar. Her sentences can be read like a dance, or a knot. Rarely does she get to the point in her prose, which may be why the endings for some of her poems appear so abrupt: *This is how life goes. . . . Give me the strength to keep living. . . . The great silence cuts the thread.* If one reveals "who" and not "what" one is through speaking and acting in the world, as Arendt argued in *The Human Condition*, then in these poems Arendt reveals herself to be a romantic at heart, and a bit of a sentimentalist. This is surprising—or not—depending on any expectations one has formed from reading her work, which criticizes romanticism, banishes feelings from the public realm, and otherwise eschews emotions as being irrational. Arendt herself was a very feeling woman, as she wrote in an early letter to her husband, "And about the love of others who branded me as cold hearted, I always thought: If only you knew how dangerous love would be for me." It is my hope that these poems, which belonged to her inner private life, add to the complex portrait of a great thinker for our times. From the girlish exuberance to the focused intensity of her later life, the poems show Arendt building a home in the world for herself, while always returning to her mother tongue.

When the commentator Günter Gaus asked Arendt on German national television what remained of Europe for her after the war, she said:

What remains? The language remains... I have always consciously refused to lose my mother tongue. I have always maintained a certain distance from French, which I then spoke very well, as well as from English, which I write today... There is a tremendous difference between your mother tongue and another language. For myself I can put it extremely simply: In German I know a rather large part of German poetry by heart; the poems are always somehow in the back of my mind. I can never do that again.[19]

A few months before her death in 1975, Arendt returned to Germany one last time. She carried a collection of her papers and notebooks with her, to be placed in the German Literature Archive in Marbach. As the coexecutor of Karl Jaspers's estate, she was tasked with organizing his correspondence for publication. It was a busy and difficult time for her. When she arrived she was in high spirits despite being in poor health, recovering from her second heart attack during the course of an international speaking tour while trying to write *The Life of the Mind*. As she emerged from the darkness of the reading room on her first day sorting papers, she made her way upstairs to the cafeteria, where she stood up in the middle of the sunlit lunchroom and recited Friedrich Schiller by heart in German to everyone's applause. (The archive sits next to the Schiller Museum, which surely delighted Arendt, who had committed many of his poems to memory.) In many ways, the trip was a homecoming for Arendt, the girl from a foreign land returned after thirty-five years gone.

All of Hannah Arendt's poems were written in German. It has not been lost on me, in translating them, that for her they were untranslatable. Because after everything, what remained for Arendt was the language of German poetry.

xxx

Notes

1. Hannah Arendt, "Prologue," in *Responsibility and Judgment*, ed. Jerome Kohn (New York: Schocken Books, 2003), 3–14.
2. Ibid.
3. Hannah Arendt's copy of Robert Lowell's *Notebook 1967–68*, with inscription and marginalia, is located in the Hannah Arendt Collection at Stevenson Library at Bard College in Annandale-on-Hudson, New York.
4. Elisabeth Young-Bruehl, *Hannah Arendt: For Love of the World* (New Haven, CT: Yale University Press, 1982).
5. Hannah Arendt and Heinrich Blücher, *Within Four Walls: The Correspondence Between Hannah Arendt and Heinrich Blücher, 1936–1968*, ed. Lotte Kohler (New York: Harcourt, 2000), 59.
6. Hannah Arendt and Karl Jaspers, *Hannah Arendt Karl Jaspers Correspondence: 1926–1969*, ed. Lotte Kohler and Hans Saner, trans. Robert and Rita Kimber (New York: Harcourt, 1992), 16.
7. Hannah Arendt, *Thinking Without a Banister: Essays in Understanding, 1953–1975*, ed. Jerome Kohn (New York: Schocken Books, 2018).
8. Some of these details come from Kathleen B. Jones, "Hannah Arendt's Female Friends," *Los Angeles Review of Books*, Nov. 12, 2013.
9. John Corry, "About New York: The West Side Intellectuals," *New York Times*, February 6, 1974.
10. Papers. Correspondence, 1938–1976; General, 1938–1976; "Bi-Bl" miscellaneous, 1960–1975, undated. Library of Congress, Washington, D.C.
11. Hannah Arendt, *Men in Dark Times* (New York: Harcourt, 1968), 263–64.
12. Robert Lowell, "On Hannah Arendt," *New York Review of Books*, May 13, 1976.
13. In 1961, after nearly a decade of friendship, Lowell dedicated his "finest poem" to Arendt. Titled "Pigeons (For Hannah Arendt)," the poem is a loose translation of Rilke's last poem, "Taube, die draussen blieb," reportedly written from his deathbed. This was an important poem for Arendt, one that she copied out lines from in her notebooks. It captures the ancient struggle between the longing for home and the desire for flight.
14. W. H. Auden, "Thinking What We Are Doing," *Encounter* 12 (June 1959): 74.
15. These essays appear in *Men in Dark Times*.
16. Hannah Arendt, *The Human Condition* (Chicago: University of Chicago Press, 1998), 169.
17. W. H. Auden, "In Memory of W.B. Yeats," *Another Time* (New York: Random House, 1940).
18. Samantha Rose Hill, "In the Archive with Hannah Arendt," Nov. 12, 2019.
19. *Zur Person*, ZDF, Oct. 28, 1964; transcribed as "What Remains? Language Remains: A Conversation with Günter Gaus," trans. Joan Stambaugh, in Hannah Arendt, *Essays in Understanding, 1930–1954* (Schocken Books, 2005).

A Note on the Translation

The poems in this volume have been gathered from three sources: the Hannah Arendt Archive at the Library of Congress in Washington, D.C.; Arendt's published correspondence; and her notebooks, which are housed at the German Literature Archive in Marbach, Germany.

The poems written between 1923 and 1942 that Arendt left to the Library of Congress appear at the end of Elisabeth Young-Bruehl's biography, *Hannah Arendt: For Love of the World* (1982). Several of the poems have also been published in Arendt's correspondence, including *Within Four Walls: The Correspondence Between Hannah Arendt and Heinrich Blücher, 1936–1968* (2000) and her correspondence with Heidegger published in *Letters: 1925–1975* (2003). The poems collected from Arendt's notebooks were published in the *Denktagebuch, 1950–1973* (2003).

There are seventy-one poems in this volume. They date from 1923 to 1961. There are no recorded poems between 1926 and 1942. These were significant years in Arendt's life. In the fall–winter of 1925 she ended her romantic relationship with Martin Heidegger, and 1942 was the beginning of her life in America after nine years in exile. The first poem that appears after the break was written in 1942 and dedicated to Walter Benjamin. As she fled to America from France in 1941, Arendt stopped in Portbou, Spain, where Benjamin tragically had taken his life a year prior. Arendt returned to Germany in November 1949. She began keeping her notebooks in 1951 after she returned to America. The poems have been separated into two parts to mark these turns in Arendt's life.

In New York, Arendt organized and typed up the poems she wrote between 1923–1926 and in 1942. The poems were handwritten in pencil on loose-leaf paper. She organized them chronologically by season. I have followed her organization method.

When Arendt collected her poems, she did not include all of them. The omitted poems have been included here. As best as I can judge from her correspondence, the omitted poems were sent directly to Martin Heidegger.

Additionally, there are variations of several poems. I have chosen to publish the last version of each and have noted the differences between versions where they occur. Alternate versions and translations can be found in Appendix A.

Translating Arendt's poems has felt like an ongoing conversation with good friends. What began as a discussion in the archive, trying to understand Arendt's relationships to poets and poems, led to conversations with friends and mentors who, over the years, have had a hand in shaping these translations. In the final stages, it has been a pleasure to work with Genese Grill and Haley Bracken, polishing Arendt's poems for appearance in the world.

Writing poems is a way of translating thinking into something that can appear in the world, and all literary translations are a series of decisions, compromises, losses, and gains. Several of

Arendt's poems were written in a rhyme scheme, which required deciding between the rhyme scheme and the content of the poem. In these instances, meaning has been given priority, but not without acknowledging that a rhyme scheme can also be a vehicle for meaning.

Arendt delighted in the play of the German language, some of which is not afforded by the English language. As such, I have made notations where we stray from the more direct or literal meaning of Arendt's language choices.

Since I began working on Arendt's poems in 2010, three volumes have appeared: one in French from Payot, *Heureux celui qui n'a pas de patrie, Poèmes de pensée*, in 2015, translated by François Mathieu and edited by Karin Biro; one in German, *Ich selbst, auch ich tanze: Die Gedichte* from Piper in 2016; and one in Spanish, from Herder Editorial in 2017, titled *Poemas* and translated by Alberto Ciria Cusculluela.

PART I

———◆———

1923-1926

Kein Wort bricht ins Dunkel—
Kein Gott hebt die Hand—
Wohin ich auch blicke
Sich türmendes Land.
Keine Form, die sich löset,
Kein Schatten, der schwebt.
Und immer noch hör ich's:
Zu spät, zu spät.

No word breaks the dark —
No god lifts a hand—
Wherever I look
This tremendous land.

No shadow hovers,
No form has weight.

And still I hear:
Too late, too late.

This poem echoes Genesis 1:2, Deuteronomy 4:11, and Rainer Maria Rilke's *Duino Elegies*, which was published in 1923. The opening line of Rilke's "First Elegy" reads, "Wer, wenn ich schriee, hörte mich denn aus der Engel Ordnungen?" (Who, if I cried out, would hear me among the angel's orders?) In a later published essay, Arendt discusses being heard by God in Rilke's poem as "Im-Hören-sein," or "being-in-hearing."

IM VOLKSLIEDTON

Sehn wir uns wieder,
Blüht weisser Flieder,
Ich hüll Dich in Kissen,
Du sollst nichts mehr missen.

Wir wollen uns Freun,
Dass herber Wein,
Dass duftende Linden
Uns noch beisammen finden.

Wenn Blätter fallen,
Dann lass uns scheiden.
Was nützt unser Wallen?
Wir müssen es leiden.

IN THE TUNE OF A FOLKSONG

We'll see each other soon,
When white lilacs bloom,
I'll make a soft bed
For you to rest your head.

We'll have a joyful time,
Drinking young wine,
With the sweet linden tree,
Still shading you and me.

When the leaves fall,
Then let us part.
What use is wallowing?
We must keep heart.

Arendt is imitating a traditional German folksong. For examples of German folksongs Arendt probably would have been familiar with, see *Des Knaben Wunderhorn* ("The Boy's Magic Horn"), a collection of German folksongs published by Achim von Arnim and Clemens Brentano in three volumes between 1805 and 1808; and Ludwig Uhland's *Alte hoch- und niederdeutsche Volkslieder* ("High and Low German Folksongs"), published in 1866, as well as his essay on German Volkslieder. Arendt had piano lessons as a child, but in the words of her mother, she did not have much ability for music.

TROST

Es kommen die Stunden,
Da alte Wunden,
Die längst vergessen,
Drohn zu zerfressen.

Es kommen die Tage,
Da keine Waage
Des Lebens, der Leiden
Sich kann entscheiden.

Die Stunden verrinnen,
Die Tage vergehen,
Es bleibt ein Gewinnen:
Das blosse Bestehen.

CONSOLATION

There come hours
When old wounds,
Long forgotten,
Threaten to devour.

There come days
When no scale
Can decide:
Life or sorrow.

The hours elapse,
The days pass,
One victory remains:
Survival.

TRAUM

Schwebende Füsse in pathetischem Glanze.

Ich selbst,

Auch ich tanze,

Befreit von der Schwere

Ins Dunkle, ins Leere

Gedrängte Räume vergangener Zeiten

Durchshrittene Weiten,

Verlorene Einsamkeiten

Beginnen zu tanzen, zu tanzen

Ich selbst,

Auch ich tanze.

Ironisch vermessen,

Ich hab nichts vergessen,

Ich kenne die Leere,

Ich kenne die Schwere,

Ich tanze, ich tanze

In ironischem Glanze

DREAM

Floating feet in lofty splendor
I myself,
I'm dancing too,
Freed from the burdens
Into the dark, into the void.

Crowded rooms of yesteryear,
Paced expanses,
Lost loneliness,
Beginning to dance, to dance

I myself,
I'm dancing too.
Ironically foolish,
I've forgotten nothing,
I know the emptiness,
I know the burden,
I dance, I dance
In ironic splendor

Dancing appears in Friedrich Nietzsche's books *The Gay Science, Ecce Homo,* and *Thus Spoke Zarathustra.* In *The Gay Science,* in an aphorism titled "The Consciousness of Appearance," Nietzsche writes, "Appearance is for me that which lives and is effective and goes so far in its self-mockery that it makes me feel that this is appearance and will-o'-the-wisp and a dance of spirits and nothing more—that among all these dreamers, I, too, who 'know,' am dancing my dancing . . ." In another: "I really do not know what the spirit of a philosopher might wish more to be than a good dancer." In *Ecce Homo,* Nietzsche describes his Zarathustra as a dancer, and in *Thus Spoke Zarathustra,* the Prophet counsels Zarathustra in his existential *Angst* to dance: "You will have to dance, lest you fall over!"

MÜDIGKEIT

Dämmernder Abend—
Leise verklagend
Tönt noch der Vögel Ruf
Die ich erschuf.

Graue Wände
Fallen hernieder,
Meine Hände
Finden sich wieder.

Was ich geliebt
Kann ich nicht fassen,
Was mich umgibt
Kann ich nicht lassen.

Alles versinkt.
Dämmern steigt auf.
Nichts mich bezwingt—
Ist wohl des Lebens Lauf.

WEARINESS

Night falling—
Birds calling
A quiet lament,
A song I made.

Gray walls
Collapse to the floor,
My hands grasp
Each other once more.

I can no longer hold
What I used to love,
I can no longer escape
What imprisons me.

Everything fades.
Dawn rises.
Nothingness conquers me—
It's just life's way.

It is possible that Arendt sent a version of this poem to Martin Heidegger in the summer of 1925. In a letter dated July 9, 1925, Heidegger wrote, "But I may be permitted to ask you, dear, not to fear such 'weary' hours and days, and not to let them become something for you only, something that does not belong to me as well . . . am I any less close to you when I am sad about your weariness?" Heidegger often quoted lines from Arendt's letters and poems back to her in his missives.

DIE UNTERGRUNDBAHN

Aus Dunkel kommend,
Ins Helle sich schlängelnd,
Schnell und vermessen,
Schmal und besessen
Von menschlichen Kräften,
Aufmerksam webend
Gezeichnete Wege,
Gleichgültig schwebend
Über dem Hasten,
Schnell schmal und bessessen
Von menschlichen Kräften,
Die es nicht achtet,
Ins Dunkle fliessend
Um Oberes wissend
Fliegt es sich windend
Ein gelbes Tier.

THE SUBWAY

Out of the darkness,
Snaking toward light,
Swift and ablaze,
Narrow and crazed,
By will of humanity,
Weaving mechanically
Rushing past,
Its designated path,
Indifferently rocking,
Swift narrow and crazed,
By will of humanity,
Acting accordingly
Flying toward darkness,
Knowing all that's above,
Writhing, released:
A yellow beast.

The Berlin S-Bahn began service on August 8, 1924. U-Bahn stands for Unter-grundbahn, or "underground railroad," and S-Bahn stands for Schnellbahn, or "rapid city rail." The S-Bahn runs aboveground except in the center of the city. In 1924, Arendt was living in Berlin and taking classes at the University of Berlin as she prepared to formally enter university.

ABSCHIED

Nun lasst mich, o schwebende Tage, die Hände Euch reichen.
Ihr entfliehet mir nicht, es gibt kein Entweichen
Ins Leere und Zeitenlose.

Doch legt eines glühenden Windes fremderes Zeichen
Sein Wehen um mich; ich will nicht entweichen
In die Leere gehemmter Zeiten.

Ach, Ihr kanntet das Lächeln, mit dem ich mich schenkte.
Ihr wusstet, wie vieles ich schweigend verhängte,
Um auf Wiesen zu liegen, und Euch zu gehören.

Doch jetzt ruft das Blut, das nimmer verdrängte
Hinaus mich auf Schiffe, die niemals ich lenkte.
Der Tod ist im Leben, ich weiss, ich weiss.

So lasst mich, o schwebende Tage, die Hände Euch reichen.
Ihr verlieret mich nicht. Ich lass Euch zum Zeichen
Dies Blatt und die Flamme zurück.

PARTING

O, vanishing days! Give me your hands.
You cannot escape me; there will be no release
Into that void of infinite time.

Even if the wind, hot and strange,
warns me away, I will not release you
Into the void of finite time.

Oh, you knew the smile with which I gave myself to you.
You knew how much I had to keep secret,
Just to lie in the meadows and be with you.

But the blood, ever restless, calls me now
To board ships I've never steered.
Death is in life, I know, I know.

O, vanishing days! Give me your hands.
You cannot lose me. I will leave you a sign:
This page and a flame behind.

Geh durch Tage ohne Richt.
Spreche Worte ohne Wicht.
Leb im Dunkeln ohne Sicht.

Bin im Leben ohne Steuer

Über mir nur Ungeheuer
Wie ein grosser schwarzer neuer
Vogel: Das Gesicht der Nacht.

Go through days without right.
Speak words without weight.
Live in darkness without sight.

I'm in life without a helm

Above me only this vastness,
Like a new dark black bird:
The face of night.

AN . . .

Nimm meiner Wünsche schwere Last.
Das Leben ist weit und ohne Hast.
Es gibt viel Länder der Welt.
Und viele Nächte im Zelt.
    Wer weiss denn eine Waage
    Des Lebens der Leiden?
    Vielleicht wird in späten Tagen
    Sich dies alles scheiden.

TO . . .

Hold the weight of my desire.
Life is long without relief.
There are so many lands in this world.
And so many nights under stars.

> Does anyone have a scale
> That can measure life's suffering?
> Maybe when we're older
> All will be decided.

Das ist nicht Glück,

Wie die es meinen,

Die betteln, weinen,

Und zu Tempeln streben

Und von dem Vorhof aus die Andacht sehen,

Und eine Weihe, die sie nicht verstehen

Mit bösem Blick sich wenden dann zurück

Und klagen über ein verlorenes Leben.

Was ist Glück dem,

Der mit sich selbst geeint ist,

Des Fuss nur stösst,

Wo es für ihn gemeint ist.

Für den Sich-Kennen Grenze ist und Recht,

Für den Sich-Nennen Zeichen im Geschlecht.

This is not happiness,
Like they think,
The begging, crying,
And striving toward temples.
From the threshold they watch the benediction,
Though they've no conception of the consecration.
And then with an evil eye they turn,
Clamoring after their own lost lives.

What is happiness for the man,
Who is pleased with himself,
Whose foot only stomps
Where it's meant to stomp.
For whom self-knowledge is boundary and right,
For whom self-naming is the badge of inheritance.

DÄMMERUNG

Dämmerung, Sinkende,
Harrende, Winkende,—

Grau ist die Flut.

Dämmerung, Schweigende,
Lautlos Dich Neigende,
Mahnende, Klagende,
Lautloses Sagende—

Grau ist die Flut.

Dämmerung, Tröstende,
Mildernde, Heilende,
Dunkles Weisende,
Neues Umkreisende,—

Grau ist die Flut.

DUSK

Dusk sinks,
Abiding, beckoning—

Gray is the flood.

Dusk, silently,
Soundlessly sinking,
Reminding, lamenting,
Soundlessly saying—

Gray is the flood.

Dusk, consoling,
Soothing, healing,
Revealing darkness—
Encountering newness—

Gray is the flood.

IN SICH VERSUNKEN

Wenn ich meine Hand betrachte
– Fremdes Ding mit mir verwandt—
Stehe ich in keinem Land,
Bin an kein Hier und Jetzt
Bin an kein Was gesetzt.

Dann ist mir als sollte ich die Welt verachten,
Mag doch ruhig die Zeit vergehen.
Nur sollen keine Zeichen mehr geschehen.

Betracht ich meine Hand,
Unheimlich nah mir verwandt.
Und doch ein ander Ding.
Ist sie mehr als ich bin
Hat sie höheren Sinn?

LOST IN MYSELF

When I consider my hand
—A foreign thing related to me—
I stand in no country,
I am neither here nor there
I am not certain of anything.

Then it seems to me I should scorn the world,
Let time slip quietly away,
As long as no more signs should appear.

I look at my hand,
It's uncannily near to me.
And yet a foreign thing.
Is it more myself than I am?
Does it have higher meaning?

SOMMERLIED

Durch des Sommers reife Fülle
Lass ich meine Hände gleiten.
Meine Glieder schmerzhaft weiten
Zu der dunklen, schweren Erde.

Felder, die sich tönend neigen
Pfade, die der Wald verschüttet
Alles zwingt zum strengen Schweigen:
Dass wir lieben, wenn wir leiden,

Dass das Opfer, dass die Fülle
Nicht des Priesters Hand verdorre,
Dass in edler klarer Stille
Uns die *Freude* nicht ersterbe.

Denn die Wasser fliessen über,
Müdigkeit will uns zerstören
Und wir lassen unser Leben
Wenn wir lieben, wenn wir leben.

SUMMER SONG

My fingers slip across
Summer's ripe fullness.
As my body aches opening
Toward the dark, heavy earth.

Fields—where no one can hear us.
Woods—where no one can see us.
All is held in strict silence.
We suffer when we love.

So that this offering, this fullness
Will not mortify the priest's hand:
And in the anointed quiet
Our *pleasure* will not die.

But exhaustion wants to destroy us
When we lose ourselves there,
And the waters overflow,
When we love, when we live.

In a letter dated May 13, 1925, Heidegger thanks Arendt for her poems, imply-
ing that she sent multiple. A week later, he wrote, "And in my rare breaks, I read
your poems. But my longing for you is becoming less and less controllable." It
is impossible to say with certainty which poems he is referring to in his letters.
While Arendt kept all of Heidegger's letters and poems, unfortunately he did
not keep any of her missives.

Warum gibst Du mir die Hand
Scheu und wie geheim?
Kommst Du aus so fernem Land,
Kennst nicht unseren Wein?

Kennst nicht unsere schönste Glut
—Lebst Du so allein?—
Mit dem Herzen, mit dem Blut
Eins im andern sein?

Weisst Du nicht des Tages Freuden,
Mit dem Liebsten gehen?
Weisst Du nicht des Abends Scheiden,
Ganz in Schwermut gehen?

Komm mit mir und hab mich lieb,
Denk nicht an dein Graun,
Kannst Du Dich denn nicht vertraun,
Komm und nimm und gib.

Gehen dann durchs reife Feld
—Mohn und wilder Klee—
Später in der weiten Welt
Tut es uns wohl weh,

Wenn wir spüren, wie im Wind
Stark Erinnerung weht.
Wenn im Schauder, traumhaft lind
Unsere Seele weht.

Why do you give your hand to me
Shy and like a secret?
Do you come from such a faraway land,
That you do not know our wine?

Don't you know our warm glow
—Do you live so alone?—
Are the heart and the blood
So different from one another?

Do you not know the day's joys
Walking with a beloved?
Do you not know the evening's farewells,
Partings full of melancholy?

Come with me and make love to me,
Do not think about your sadness,
Can't you trust yourself—
Come and take and give.

Going then through ripe fields
—Poppy and wild clover—
Only later may it cause us pain

When we sense how in the wind
Memories strongly flow.
When in their shudder, soft and dreamlike
Our souls move.

ABSCHIED

Du gibst uns die Trauer, dass nichts uns verweilet,
Und schenkst uns die Hoffnung, wie Vieles sich eilet.
Du bist uns das Zeichen für Freude und Schmerzen
Du zeigst uns die Wege und öffnest die Herzen.

Du fügest zusammen, wie nie unsere Hände
Wir glauben an Treue und fühlen die Wende
Wir können nicht sagen, wie sehr wir uns einen.
Wir können nur weinen.

GOODBYE

You bring us sadness—nothing remains.
You give us hope—everything rushing.
You are the sign of pleasure and pain.
You show us the way and open hearts.

You join our hands together like never before,
We trust our love as we turn away,
We cannot say how much we are one,
All we can do is cry.

SPÄTSOMMER

Der Abend hat mich zugedeckt
So weich wie Samt, so schwer wie Leid.

Ich weiss nicht mehr, wie Liebe tut
Ich weiss nicht mehr der Felder Glut
Und alles will entschweben,
Um nur mir Ruh zu geben.

Ich denk an ihn und hab ihn lieb,
Doch wie aus fernem Land
Und fremd ist mir das Komm und Gib,
Kaum weiss ich, was mich bannt.

Der Abend hat mich zugedeckt
So weich wie Samt, so schwer wie Leid.
Und nirgends sich Empörung reckt
Zu Neuer Freud und Traurigkeit.

Und alles Weiter, das mich rief
Und alles Gestern klar und tief
Kann mich nicht mehr betören.

Ich weiss ein Wasser gross und fremd
Und eine Blum, die keiner nennt.
Was soll mich noch zerstören?

Der Abend hat mich zugedeckt
So weich wie Samt, so schwer wie Leid.

LATE SUMMER

The night envelops me
soft as velvet, severe as misery.

I no longer know how love hurts
I no longer know how fields burn
Everything falls away
Just to give me rest.

I think of him and how I loved him,
Like a person from a foreign land.
So strange to me this come-and-give,
I barely know how I was bewitched.

The night envelops me
soft as velvet, severe as misery.
And nothing can make my rage
into new pleasure or sadness.

And everything far away calls to me.
All the yesterdays so plain and clear
Cannot bewitch me.

I know a water vast and strange
And a bloom that no one can name.
What could hurt more?

The night envelops me
soft as velvet, severe as misery.

OKTOBER—VORMITTAG

Dies fahle Licht des Herbstes macht mich leiden
Und wenn ich langsam meine tausend Schmerzen zähle
Lässt es mein Auge trüben Blicks sich weiden
An Allem, was ich Heimlich seh und wähle

Ach wer will wägen, was er nicht erfasset –
Und wer will sagen, was erst spät sich scheidet –
Denn wie mit beiden Händen er es fasset
Weiss er nicht mehr warum er es noch leidet

OCTOBER—LATE MORNING

The pallid autumn light makes me ache
As I slowly count my thousand pains
I widen my eyes and look blearily
Upon everything I secretly see and desire.

Why? Who wants to weigh what he cannot grasp –
And who wants to say what he might later decide –
When he holds us in both hands
Even he doesn't know why he's suffering.

KLAGE

Ach, die Tage, sie verfliegen ungenützt dahin wie Spiel.
Und die Stunden, sie erliegen ungeschützt dem Qualenspiel

Und der Zeiten Auf und Nieder
Gleitet leise durch mich hin,
Und ich sing die alten Lieder,
Weiss nicht mehr als zu Beginn.

Und ein Kind kann nicht verträumter gehn den
    vorgeschrieben Gang.
Und ein Greis kann nicht geduldiger wissen, dass das Leben lang.

Doch das Leid will nicht beschwichten
Alte Träume, junge Weisheit.
Und es lässt mich nicht verzichten
Auf des Glückes schöne Reinheit.

LAMENT

Oh, the days, they waste away, like an unplayed game.
And the hours succumb to the play of torment

The time rises and falls
Slipping softly through me,
As I sing the old songs,
Knowing only the beginning.

And no child could follow her predestined path more dreamily
And no old man could know how long life is more certainly.

But sorrow will not silence
Old dreams or young wisdom.
Nor will it make me give up on
The beautiful pure joy of life.

AN DIE FREUNDE

Trauert nicht der leisen Klage,
Wenn der Blick des Heimatlosen
Scheu Euch noch umwirbt.
Fühlt, wie stolz die reinste Sage
Alles noch verbirgt.

Spürt der Dankbarkeit und Treue
Zartestes Erbeben.
Und Ihr wisst: in steter Neue
Wird die Liebe geben.

TO THE FRIENDS

Do not trust the silent lament,
When the eyes of the homeless
Shyly look to you.
Feel how their prideful stories
Conceal everything.

Feel your faith and gratitude
Gently shaken.
And know: in constant renewal
There will be love.

AN DIE NACHT

Neig Dich, Du Tröstende, leis meinem Herzen.
Schenke mir, Schweigende, Lindrung der Schmerzen.
Deck Deine Schatten vor Alles zu Helle—
Gib mir Ermatten und Flucht vor der Grelle.

Lass mir Dein Schweigen, die kühlende Löse,
Lass mich im Dunkel verhüllen das Böse.
Wenn Helle mich peinigt mit neuen Gesichten;
Gib Du mir die Kraft zum steten Verrichten.

TO THE NIGHT

Come here, Consoler, quiet my heart.
Grant me, Silencer, respite from this pain,
Cover all that's too bright with your shadows,
Give me rest and relief from the light.

Let me rest in your silence, its cooling release,
Let me shroud the evil in your darkness.
And if light torments me with new visions,
Give me the strength to remain steady.

NACHTLIED

Nur die Tage laufen weiter,
Lassen unsere Zeit verstreichen.
Stets dieselben dunklen Zeichen
Wird die Nacht uns stumm bereiten.

Sie muss stets dasselbe sagen
Auf dem gleichen Ton beharren,
Zeiget auch nach neuem Wagen
Immer nur, was wir schon waren.

Laut und fremd verlockt der Morgen,
Bricht den dunklen stummen Blick,
Gibt mit tausend neuen Sorgen
Uns dem bunten Tag zurück.

Doch die Schatten werden bleiben,
Um den Tag sich scheu zu schliessen,
Lassen wir auf raschen Flüssen
Uns zu fernen Küsten treiben.

Unsere Heimat sind die Schatten,
Und wenn wir zutiefst ermatten,
In dem nächtlich dunklen Schoss
Hoffen wir auf leisen Trost.

Hoffend können wir verzeihn
Allen Schrecken, allen Kummer.
Unsere Lippen werden stummer—
Lautlos bricht der Tag herein.

NIGHT SONG

The days lapse away,
Letting our time expire.
Still the night shows us silently
the same dark signs.

Night must always say the same thing,
Always sing the same note,
Showing in new ways
We only are what we already were.

Morning light loud and strange,
Breaks the dark and silent show,
Returning us to the colors of day
with a thousand new troubles.

And yet when the day is done
The shadows linger,
On rushing rivers let us drift
Off to distant shores.

The shadows are our home.
And when we're weak and tired,
In the dark womb of night
We hope for comfort.

We hope we can forgive
All the horrors, all the grief.
Our lips grow still—
Silently, the day breaks.

Note

No record remains of poems Hannah Arendt might have written between 1926 and 1941. Forced to flee Nazi Germany in 1933, Arendt spent nine years in exile doing political work in Paris helping Jewish youth escape to Palestine before arriving in the United States on May 22, 1941.

PART II

1942-1961

W. B.

Einmal dämmert Abend wieder,
Nacht fällt nieder von den Sternen,
Liegen wir gestreckte Glieder
In den Nähen, in den Fernen.

Aus den Dunkelheiten tönen
Sanfte kleine Melodeien.
Lauschen wir uns zu entwöhnen,
Lockern endlich wir die Reihen.

Ferne Stimmen, naher Kummer—
Jene Stimmen jener Toten,
Die wir vorgeschickt als Boten
Uns zu leiten in den Schlummer.

W. B.

Eventide descends once more,
Night falls down from the stars;
We stretch our limbs, reaching out
To those near, and those far.

Gentle whispering melodies
Sound from the darkness.
We listen so we can let go,
Finally breaking rank.

Distant voices, nearby sorrow—
The voices of those dead,
The messengers we sent ahead,
To guide us into slumber.

"W. B." stands for Walter Benjamin. This poem was written in 1942 likely after
Arendt received a printed facsimile of Benjamin's final work from Theodor
Adorno and Max Horkheimer. Benjamin had entrusted Arendt with his manu-
scripts when they parted ways in Marseille shortly before he attempted to escape
over the Pyrenees from France into Spain with the resistance fighter Lisa Fittko
in September 1940. Benjamin took his life shortly after crossing the border into
Portbou, Spain, when officials told the party they would have to return to France.
Arendt traveled to Portbou in 1941 to find his grave, which could not be found.

There is a bit of play in the German language of this poem between the first and
second stanza. The word *das Gleid* means "limb" and "link in a chain," and is echoed
in the second stanza with *die Reihen*, which means "chain," and "to close ranks."

Recht und Freiheit
Brüder zagt nicht
Vor uns scheint das Morgenrot.
Recht und Freiheit
Brüder wagt es
Morgen schlagen wir den Teufel tot.

Von den Bergen
Aus den Tälern
Schleppt am Fuss das Bleigewicht;
Recht und Freiheit
Brüder fragt nicht
Wir nun sind das Weltgericht.

Weite Länder
Enge Gassen
Brüder das ist unser Schritt.
Weinen, Lachen
Lieben Hassen
Alle Götter ziehen wir mit.

Justice and freedom
Brothers, don't hesitate
Dawn rises before us.
Justice and freedom
Brothers, take a risk
Tomorrow we strike the devil dead.

From the mountains
to the valleys
Schlepp on foot this leaden weight;
Justice and freedom
Brothers, don't ask
We're the world court now.

Wide lands
Narrow streets
Brothers, that's our fate.
Crying, laughing
Love and hate—
We're bringing all the gods with us now.

"Einigkeit und Recht und Freiheit," commonly translated as "Unity and Justice and Freedom," is the first line of the third stanza of the national anthem of Germany, "Das Lied der Deutschen."

Aufgestiegen aus dem stehenden Teich der Vergangenheit
Sind der Erinn'rungen viele.
Nebelgestalten ziehen die sehnsüchtigen Kreise
  meiner Gefangenheit
Vergangen, verlockend, am Ziele.

Tote, was wollt Ihr? Habt Ihr im Orkus nicht Heimat und Stätte?
Endlich den Frieden der Tiefe?
Wasser und Erde, Feuer und Luft sind Euch ergeben, als hätte
Mächtig ein Gott Euch. Und riefe

Euch aus stehenden Wässern, aus Sümpfen, Mooren und Teichen
Sammelnd geeinigt herbei.
Schimmernd im Zwielicht bedeckt Ihr mit Nebel der
  Lebenden Reiche,
Spottend des dunklen Vorbei.

Spielen wollen auch wir; ergreifen und lachen und haschen
Träume vergangener Zeit.
Müde wurden auch wir der Strassen, der Städte, des raschen
Wechsels der Einsamkeit.

Unter die rudernden Boote mit liebenden Paaren
  geschmückt auf
Stehenden Teichen im Wald
Könnten auch wir uns mischen – leise, versteckt und entrückt auf
Nebelwolken, die bald

There are so many memories
Rising from still ponds of the past.
Ghosts drawing circles around me,
imprisoning me, leading me on.

Ghosts, what are you doing? Is Orcus not your home?
Is there no eternal peace in the underworld?
Water and earth, fire and air are yours,
As if a mighty God held you, and called

You up from still waters, from swamps, pools and ponds,
Gathering you here.
Shimmering in twilight, cloaked in the mist of living realms,
Scornful of the dark past.

We want to play too; to grasp and laugh and steal
Dreams of past times.
We're weary too, of the streets, the cities, the sudden
Turn to loneliness.

Among the rowboats adorned with loving pairs
On still ponds in the woods,
We could blend in too—quiet, out of sight, lost
In reveries of cloud mist that

Sachte die Erde bekleiden, das Ufer, den Busch und den Baum,
Wartend des kommenden Sturms.
Wartend des aus dem Nebel, aus Luftschloss,
    Narrheit und Traum
Steigenden wirbelnden Sturms.

Gently cloak the earth, the shore, the bush and tree,
Waiting for the coming storm.
Waiting out the fog, folly, cloud castles and dreams
Rising from the whirling storm.

PARK AM HUDSON

Fischer fischen still an Flüssen
In der ganzen Welt.
Fahrer fahren blind auf Wegen
Um die ganze Welt.
Kinder laufen, Mütter rufen,
Golden liegt die Welt.
Geht ein liebend Paar vorüber
Manchmal durch die Welt.

Fischer fischen still an Flüssen
Bis zum Abendrot.
Fahrer fahren blind auf Wegen
Eilig in den Tod.
Kinder selig in der Sonne
Spielen Ewigkeit.
Manchmal geht ein Paar vorüber,
Mit ihm geht die Zeit.

Fischer fischen still an Flüssen—
Einsam hängt der Ast.
Fahrer fahren blind auf Wegen
Rastlos in die Rast.

PARK ON THE HUDSON

Fishers fish quietly on rivers
    In the world.
Drivers drive blindly on roads
    Around the world.
Children run, mothers call,
Golden is the world.
A loving pair passes by,
Sometimes through the world.

Fishers fish quietly on rivers
    Until the sun sets.
Drivers drive blindly on paths
    Swiftly toward death.
Children, blissful in the sun,
Play at eternity.
Sometimes a pair passes by,
With them goes the time.

Fishers fish quietly on rivers—
    Lonely hangs the rod.
Drivers drive blindly on paths
    Restless for rest.

When Arendt and Heinrich Blücher arrived in New York City on May 22, 1941, they rented two semifurnished rooms at 317 West 95th Street using a seventy-dollar monthly stipend from the Zionist Organization of America. Their apartment was half a block from Riverside Park.

Kinder spielen, Mütter rufen,
Ewigkeit ist fast.
Geht ein liebend Paar vorüber,
Trägt der Zeiten Last.

Children play, mothers call,
Eternity, almost—
A loving pair passes by,
Bearing the burden of Time.

When Arendt typed up this poem she added the title and changed the last two lines, which in the handwritten version read: "Selten geht ein Paar vorüber / Trägt der Zeiten Last" ("Sometimes a pair passes by, bearing the burden of time").

Die Traurigkeit ist wie ein Licht im Herzen angezündet,
Die Dunkelheit is wie ein Schein, der unsere Nacht ergründet.
Wir brauchen nur das kleine Licht der Trauer zu entzünden,
Um durch die lange weite Nacht wie Schatten heimzufinden.
Beleuchtet ist der Wald, die Stadt, die Strasse und der Baum.
Wohl dem, der keine Heimat hat; er sieht sie noch im Traum.

Mournfulness is like a flame lit in the heart,

Darkness, a light that leads us through the night.

We need only ignite our grief,

To find home in the long dark night, like shadows.

The forest is illuminated, the city, the street, and the trees.

Blessed is he who has no home; he still sees it in his dreams.

Arendt plays with Nietzsche's conception of metaphysical homelessness in the final line of this poem. In *The Gay Science*, under the heading "We Who Are Homeless," Nietzsche writes, "Among Europeans today there is no lack of those who are entitled to call themselves homeless in a distinctive and honorable sense: it is to them that I especially commend my secret wisdom and *gaya scienza*."

Ich weiss, dass die Strassen zerstört sind.
Wo leuchtet die Wagenspur, die wunderbar unversehrte
aus antiken Trümmern hervor?

Ich weiss, dass die Häuser gestürzt sind.
In sie traten wir in die Welt, wunderbar sicher, dass sie
beständiger als wir selbst.

Ob der Mond, den wir diesmal vergassen,
in seinem beständigeren Licht
der Pferde Hufe noch mitträgt
wie ein Echo aus des Flusses schweigendem Gesicht?

I know that the streets are destroyed.
Where are the wagon tracks, miraculously unscathed,
shining forth from ancient ruins?

I know that the houses have fallen.
We entered the world in them, wonderfully sure, that they
were more durable than ourselves.

We've forgotten this time—
Does the moon in its more enduring light
still bear hoof marks
like a ripple on the river's silent face?

TRAUM

Zwei Latten im Zaun,
zwei Wurzeln im Wald,
zwei Bäume verneigen sich
vor der Gestalt.

Im Rücken der Graben
und rechts das Gehege.
Die Lichtung entsteigt
der Biegung am Wege.

Vor mir die Wiese,
vor mir die Helle.
Woher kommt nur diese
vertrauteste Stelle?

Zwei Latten im Zaun,
zwei Wurzeln im Wald,
zwei Bäume bezeugen
des Traumes Gewalt.

DREAM

Two slats in the fence
two roots in the forest
two trees bow down
before a figure.

In the back, the ditch,
an enclosure on the right.
The clearing appears
at the bend in the path.

Before me the meadow,
before me a brightness.
But whence comes
this familiar place?

Two roots in the wood
two slats in the fence,
two trees bear witness
to the dream's Violence.

Fluch:

In jeder Frau wirst Du mich misskennen,
in jeder Gestalt vergeblich mich nennen,
in jeder Ferne wirst Nähe Du wittern,
in jeder Ruhe wird Deine Hand zittern.

Und so kommt das Ende. Unendlich geschieden,
nicht morgen, nicht gestern, nicht heute. Hienieden
ist alles verwirkt in Gezeiten;
Die warten unendlich auf leere Jenseitigkeiten.

Antwort.

In jeder Frau hab ich Dich misskannt,
in jeder Gestalt Dich vergeblich genannt,
in jeder Ferne Dich nah gewittert,
in jeder Ruhe hat meine Hand gezittert.

Doch wenn das Ende gekommen sein wird,
werd ich Deiner nicht mehr gedenken.
Und wenn das Jenseits zu öd ohne Dich ist,
dann komm ich zurück mich ertränken.

Curse:

You will call every woman by my name,
You will mistake every shape for me in vain,
You will sense my nearness in every distance,
Your hand will tremble in every stillness.

This is how the end comes. Infinitely parted.
Not tomorrow, not yesterday, not today. Here in the world
We forfeit all to the tides
Endlessly waiting for an empty afterlife.

Reply:

I called every woman by your name,
I mistook every shape for you in vain,
I sensed your nearness in every distance,
My hand trembled in every stillness.

But when the end comes,
I'll think of you no more.
And if the afterlife is too lonely without you,
Then I'll return to drown myself.

Herr der Nächte—
Dunkelgolden
Glänzt Du abends aus dem Strome,
wenn ich von dem Hügel
laufend lechze
mich zu betten in die Kühle.

Herr der Nächte—
Voller Unduld
harr ich Deines Traums, der Nacht.
Tag an Tag reiht sich
zur Kette,
die doch jeder Abend sprengt.

Herr der Nächte—
Schlag die Brücke
von den Ufern übern Strom.
Dass ich, wenn ich von dem Hügel
laufend lechze
mich zu betten in die Kühle,
noch im letzten Sprung mich fange
auf der Brücke,
zwischen Ufern, zwischen Tagen
Überm Glanze Deines Golds.

Lord of the nights—
Dark, golden
You gleam, evenings off the river,
When I descend,
Yearning from heights,
To bask in cool delight.

Lord of the nights—
Rife with impatience
I abide by your dream, the night.
Day follows day,
Links in a chain
That burst every evening.

Lord of the nights—
Forge the bridge
Between shores above the river
So that I, when descending,
Yearning from heights,
To bask in cool delight,
Can catch myself on the way—
The last leap on the bridge
Between shores, between days,
Across your golden splendor.

Arendt enclosed this in a letter to her husband on July 21, 1947, along with poems by Hermann Broch and Theodor Sapper, so he would have something from his "own personal poet." He replied on July 25: "The poem by my own personal poet is very nice, even though I don't quite understand it; but it has a nocturnal grace and makes a strong impression. There is so much of you in it, one can really see you run." Arendt later made several edits to the poem.

Ich bin ja nur ein kleiner Punkt
nicht grösser als der schwarze
der dort auf dem Papiere prunkt
als Anfang zum Quadrate.

Wenn ich mich sehr erweitern will,
beginn ich sehr zu klecksen,
mit Stift und Feder, Blei und Tint
die Umwelt zu behexen.

Doch bin ich nur ein kleiner Punkt
nicht einmal gut geraten,
wie der auf den Papieren prunkt
als Anfang zu Quadraten.

I am just a little point
no more than a spot
a black prick upon the page
like the beginning of a square.

When I start to spread
I begin to wildly splatter
with pencil and lead, quill and ink
cursing the whole world.

But I am just a little point
not even very round,
a spot that pricks the page,
like the beginning of a square.

Dies war der Abschied:
Manche Freunde kamen mit
und wer nicht mitkam war ein Freund nicht mehr.

Dies war der Abend.
Zögernd senkte er den Schritt
und zog zum Fenster unsere Seelen raus.

Dies war der Zug.
Vermass das Land im Fluge
und stockte durch die Enge mancher Stadt.

Dies ist die Ankunft.
Brot heisst Brot nicht mehr
und Wein in fremder Sprache ändert das Gespräch.

This was the farewell:
Many friends came with us
and whoever did not come was no longer a friend.

This was the evening:
Haltingly, it slowed our pace,
and drew our souls out the window.

This was the train:
Measuring the country in flight
and slowing as it passed through many cities.

This is the arrival:
Bread is no longer called bread
and wine in a foreign language changes the conversation.

This poem echoes Friedrich Hölderlin's "Brot und Wein" ("Bread and Wine"), which was written in 1801.

Nüchtern-mystisch, mystisch-nüchtern,
Anders ist es nicht zu machen:
Darum ist dein Wissen schüchtern,
Deine Schüchternheit dein Wachen.

Dry-drunken, drunken-dry,
It cannot be otherwise:
This is why your knowledge is shy;
Your shyness is your disguise.

Unaufhörlich führt uns der Tag hinweg von dem Einen
Das in gesammelter Kraft eben noch stand in der Tür.

Unaufhörlich schlagen Türen ins Schloss und
  Brücken versinken
in den strömenden Strom, hat sie Dein Fuss kaum berührt.

Incessantly the day distracts us from the One
That just now stood in the doorway with gathered strength.
Incessantly doors slam in castles and bridges sink into
    flooding streams
At the slightest touch of your foot.

Manchmal aber kommt es hervor, das Vertrauteste, öffnet die
Tore des Hauses und steht, ewiges Bleiben im Spurt.
Wie die Brücke sich schwingt über Ströme von Unrast, von
    Ufer zu Ufer,
Sicher verbunden, festes Gebild, Freiheit und Heimat in eins.

Sometimes the most familiar one comes and opens
The door to the house and stands, suspended in motion.
Like the bridge that swings over streams of unrest, from
    shore to shore,
Securely fastened, strongly built, freedom and home in one.

Flüsse ohne Brücke
Häuser ohne Wand
Wenn der Zug durchquert es—
Alles unerkannt

Menschen ohne Schatten
Arme ohne Hand

Rivers without bridges
Houses without walls
When the train flies through—
Everything unrecognizable.

People without shadows
Arms without a hand

This poem from 1950 does not appear in Arendt's hand-collected poems. It was written inside her copy of Ernst Jünger's war diaries. Arendt received the book as a present from Johannes Zilkens, a doctor, on her first return trip to Germany. Zilkens's dedication is dated "February 28, 1950, Cologne." You can see the digitized copy of Arendt's copy in the Stevenson Library at Bard College at https://www.bard.edu/library/pdfs/archives/2023/06/Junger-Strahlungen.pdf.

Was wir sind und scheinen,
Ach wen geht es an.
Was wir tun und meinen,
Niemand stoss' sich dran.

Himmel steht in Flammen,
Hell das Firmament
Über dem Beisammen,
Das den Weg nicht kennt.

Oh, who cares
What we are and how we appear.
It doesn't make a difference to them,
What we do or think.

The sky is in flames,
Heaven is on fire
Above us all,
Who don't know the way.

I

Unermessbar, Weite, nur,
wenn wir zu messen trachten,
was zu fassen unser Herz hier ward bestellt.

Unergründlich, Tiefe, nur,
wenn wir ergründend loten,
was uns Fallende als Grund empfängt.

Unerreichbar, Höhe, nur,
wenn unsere Augen mühsam absehn,
was als Flamme übersteigt das Firmament.

Unentrinnbar, Tod, nur,
wenn wir zukunftsgierig
eines Augenblickes reines Bleiben nicht ertragen.

II

Komm und wohne
in der schrägen, dunklen Kammer meines Herzens,
dass der Wände Weite noch zum Raum sich schliesst.

Komm und falle
in die bunten Gründe meines Schlafes,
der sich ängstigt vor des Abgrunds Steile unserer Welt.

I

Distance is only unmeasurable
when we cut away at
what our hearts are fastened to.

Depths are only unfathomable
when we fathom the ground,
that catches us when we've fallen.

Heights are only unimaginable
when our eyes imagine,
flames devouring the sky.

Death is only unescapable
when we're hungry for the future
and can't bear the present.

II

Come and dwell
in the dark beveled chamber of my heart,
as its walls widen to become a room.

Come and fall
in the colorful fields of my dreams,
fearful of the steep abyss that is our world.

Komm und fliege
in die ferne Kurve meiner Sehnsucht,
dass der Brand aufleuchte in die Höhe *einer* Flamme

Steh und bleibe.
Warte, dass die Ankunft unentrinnbar
zukommt aus dem Zuwurf eines Augenblicks.

Come and fly
along the vast curves of my longing,
until the fire rises to the height of *a* blaze.

Stand and stay.
Wait, as the inescapable future
comes from the thrownness of a moment.

along the vast curves of my longing: Arendt borrows a line from Rilke. In an untitled poem marked "Venice mid-July 1912," he wrote: "O die Kurven meiner Sehnsucht durch das Weltall . . ." ("O the curves of my longing through the cosmos").

There are two additional versions of this poem, one from May 2, 1951, and the other from June 4, 1951. The word "thrownness" in the last line is a translation of the German "Zuwurf," which was used by Heidegger to describe one's existential state in the world: "Zuwurf des Seyns," or the "throw of being."

Die Gedanken kommen zu mir,
ich bin ihnen nicht mehr fremd.
Ich wachse ihnen als Stätte zu
wie ein gepflügtes Feld.

The thoughts come to me,
I'm no longer a stranger to them.
I grow into their dwelling
like a plowed field.

This poem engages with Heidegger's *Erfahrung des Denkens,* in which he writes, "Wir kommen nie zu Gedanken. Sie kommen zu uns. Das ist die schickliche Stunde des Gesprächs." ("We never come to thoughts. Thoughts come to us. This is the proper hour for conversation.")

This poem is reproduced verbatim in another handwritten version dated June 3, 1951.

H. B.

Überleben.

Wie aber lebt man mit den Toten? Sag,
wo ist der Laut, der Ihren Umgang schwichtet,
wie die Gebärde, wenn durch sie gerichtet,
wir wünschen, dass die Nähe selbst sich uns versagt.

Wer weiss die Klage, die sie uns entfernt
und zieht den Schleier vor das leere Blicken?
Was hilft, dass wir uns in ihr Fort-sein schicken,
und dreht das Fühlen um, das Überleben lernt.

H. B.

Survival.

But how does one live with the dead? Say,

where is the sound of their company,

where are the gestures they once made?

We wish to be near to them, but cannot.

Who knows the lament that took him from us

and drew the veil before his empty gaze?

What helps? That we offer ourselves to them,

and turning this feeling around, learn to survive.

This poem appears in one of Arendt's notebooks. She made a number of edits to the initial draft, which included an extra line at the end: "Das umgedrehte Fühlen ist doch wie der Dolch, den man im Herzen umdreht." ("But the turned-around feeling is like a dagger one turns in one's heart.") The entry on the next page in Arendt's notebook is an aching reflection on Hermann Broch's death. Arendt met Broch shortly after she went to work for Schocken Books in 1946. Broch died suddenly of a heart attack in the spring of 1951. In a letter to Alfred Kazin, echoing her poem, Arendt writes, "Broch's death was a sudden and deep shock—He belonged even more to my world than I had realized while he was still alive. I last saw him two days before his death—in my office where he used to come and fetch me for a cup of tea at Childs'. And here, right besides [sic] this typewriter, is the couch on which he used to sleep. I somehow can't get reconciled to his being dead forever. You see, I am really hurt. First because, as one of my more lovely acquaintances in this country put it, 'I take this sort of thing (meaning death) so seriously' (is not that lovely?), and second because I begin to realize how many of my very best friends are between 60 and 70. I'm up against the problem of 'surviving,' which is the vulgar version of the more serious question: How does one live with the dead? It is obvious, isn't it, that one needs new feelings, new manners, new everything. . . . Think of me, sitting in a corner, very quiet, and pondering the problem of 'surviving.' "

Ach, wie die
Zeit sich eilt,
unverweilt
Jahr um Jahr
an ihre
Kette reiht.
Ach, wie bald
ist das Haar
weiss und verweht.

Doch, wenn die
Zeit sich teilt
jählings in
Tag und Nacht,
wenn uns das
Herz verweilt—
spielt es nicht
mit der Zeit
Ewigkeit.

Oh, how the
time passes,
relentless,
year after year
adding links
to its chain.
Oh, how soon
is the hair
white and gone.

Yet, if the
time divides
quickly into
day and night,
Then when our
heart rests—
It doesn't play
with the time
forever.

This undated poem appears after Arendt's reflections on Hermann Broch's sudden death and is reproduced verbatim in her notebook on August 6, 1951.

Nur wem der Sturz im Flug sich fängt,
gehen die Gründe auf.
Ihm steigen sie herrlich ans Licht.

Die Erde, wem der Flug misslingt,
öffnet die Abgründe weit.
Ihn nimmt sie zurück in den Schloss.

Only for the one who transforms falling into flight
        does the ground rise up.
        For him, it rises gloriously to the light.

For the one whom flight fails, the earth
        opens its chasm wide.
        Taking him back into its chamber.

Zwei Jahre in ihren Gezeiten
Von Stunden und Tagen erfüllt.
Sie kommen und sie entgleiten
Im Gischt, der das Schiff umspült.

Erst trugen sie mich über die Wellen,
Entfalteten dann gross ihren Schmerz.
Nun lassen sie mich ohne Gesellen
Zurück mit vereinsamtem Herz.

Two years in their tides
Filled up with hours and days.
They come and slip away
Like spume splattering a ship.

First they carried me over the waves,
Unfurling their great agony.
Now they leave me without company
Alone with my lonesome heart.

With a Guggenheim fellowship to work on what would become *The Human Condition*, Arendt spent the spring and summer of 1952 in Europe, conducting research in various libraries. She crossed the Atlantic by ship that March. Upon her arrival she wrote a letter to Blücher: "A quick wobbly greeting, which will be sent to you tomorrow from England. The crossing is at least as stormy as two years ago. Work, impossible. *Tant pis.* I'm letting myself be rocked up and down by the enormous breath of the sea, and am full of admiration for the man who invented the ship. . . . You can tell by my handwriting that this is a real wobble-pot. But sea and sky and clouds and sun—and nothing else—it makes one ready to accept anything."

FAHRT DURCH FRANKREICH

Erde dichtet Feld an Feld,
flicht die Bäume ein daneben,
lässt uns unsere Wege weben
um die Äcker in die Welt.

Blüten jubeln in dem Winde,
Grass schiesst auf, sie weich zu betten,
Himmel blaut und grüsst mit Linde,
Sonne spinnt die sanften Ketten.

Menschen gehen unverloren—
Erde, Himmel, Licht und Wald—
jeden Frühling neu geboren
spielend in das Spiel der Allgewalt.

DRIVE THROUGH FRANCE

Earth writes poetry field after field,
braiding the trees alongside,
letting us weave our way
through the lands of the world.

Blossoms rejoice in the wind,
Grass shoots out into soft supple beds,
Sky turns blue and greets the Linden trees,
Sun spins soft chains.

People go unlost—All are redeemed
Earth, sky, light and woods—
Reborn every spring
Playfully in the play of omnipotence.

Arendt enclosed this poem in a letter to Blücher from Paris. Dated May 1, 1952,
it begins, "My letters get to be so long because I have so much to tell you. They
could be even longer. I'm a little embarrassed. So that you know how I feel, I'll
write you a little poem, that came to me as we drove from Chartres through the
blossoming countryside." Blücher responds, "Dearest, Your letters have really
become a necessity for me, I run to the mailbox. Your voice sounds so clear
from within them, and you really give me the chance to participate a little in
Paris and Europe, and to enjoy them along with you. I can picture everything
so well again." A few days later, he added, "Your poem is as beautiful as an
Uhland spring song. I suggest changes in the following three lines: 'The sky
turns blue and mildly greets / The sun wreathes in warm chains . . . / in the
play of the gentle universal power." In the end, Arendt made only one change
to the final line of the poem, which originally read, "In the play of the most
fantastic violence."

MIT EINEM DING

Bin nur eines
von den Dingen,
den geringen,
das gelang
aus Überschwang.

Schliesse mich in Deine Hände,
dass sie schwingend
überschwingen
ins Gelingen,
wenn Dir bang ist.

WITH ONE THING

I am only one
of those things,
the low one
that won
out of ardor.

Enclose me in your hands,
as they shake
to excess
to bring you success
when you're anxious.

Arendt wrote this poem in her notebook and transcribed it on the same page as
the previous poem when she returned to New York. The only modification from
the notebook is the lowering of capital letters at the beginning of each line.

Den Überfluss ertragen
wenn Well' um Well' sich bricht,
das Zeigen sich versagen,
im Schweigen zu verharren—
O Gott, Du hörst uns nicht.

Aus Überfluss errettet
uns Gottes Stimme nicht.
Sie spricht nur zu den Darbenden,
den Sehnsüchtigen, den Harrenden.
O Gott, vergiss *uns* nicht.

Endure the abundance
when wave breaks upon wave,
refusing to appear,
to remain silent –
O God, you do not hear us.

God's voice does not save us
From the abundance.
He speaks only to the destitute,
those longing, those waiting.
O God, do not forget *us*.

Die Neige des Tages
die Schwelle des Abends
noch ist es nicht Nacht
noch hebt sich der Vogel
noch streckt sich der Baum.
Bald wehet es kälter,
die Nacht und der Traum.

The end of days
the threshold of evenings
still it is not night
still the birds take flight
still the trees stretch out.
Soon it blows cooler,
the night and the dream.

B'S GRAB

1. November.

Auf dem Hügel unter dem Baum
zwischen sinkender Sonne und steigendem Mond
Hängt Dein Grab,

Schwingt sich ein in das Totsein,
in das Sinken der Sonne,
in das Steigen des Monds.

Unter dem Himmel, über der Erde
vom Himmel herab, zum Himmel hinan
Ruht Dein Grab.

B's GRAVE

November 1

On the hill under the tree
between the setting sun and rising moon
hangs your grave,

Keeping time in a state of death,
in the setting of the sun,
in the rising of the moon.

Under the firmament, above the earth,
down from the heavens, up toward the sky
rests your grave.

"B" refers to Hermann Broch. There are two versions of this poem in Hannah Arendt's papers, one written by hand and one typed. We have translated her typed draft.

Und keine Kunde
von jenen Tagen,
die ineinander
sich brennend verzehrten
und uns versehrten:
des Glückes Wunde
wird Stigma, nicht Narbe.

Davon wär' keine Kunde,
Wenn nicht Dein Sagen
ihm Bleiben gewährte:
Gedichtetes Wort
ist Stätte, nicht Hort.

And no record
of those days
tangled into one another
devoured by flames
that burned us:
The wounds of happiness
Become stigmas, not scars.

There would be no record,
if your account
had not been imparted—
poetic language
is a place, not a refuge.

There are two versions of this poem. In the handwritten version that appears
in one of Arendt's notebooks there is an additional stanza at the end, which
Arendt cut when she typed it up. The alternate version is in Appendix A.

PALENVILLE

Spannlos winkt mir hinter gehäufeten Hügeln die Weite
Und das Ferne bricht durch, leuchtend wie Mond in der Nacht.

PALENVILLE

The distance beckons to me calmly, from behind the gathered hills
And what is far away breaks through, radiant like the moon in
the night.

Palenville is a small village at the foot of the Catskill Mountains in upstate New
York. Arendt and Blücher liked to spend their summers at the Chestnut Lawn
House in the 1950s and '60s, often staying from mid-August to mid-October,
traveling for work when necessary. This was a time of relaxation for them:
Arendt read Agatha Christie and Simenon novels and Blücher read westerns.
They spent evenings with friends enjoying drinks, visiting the pool parlor in
town, and playing chess. After Blücher suffered a series of mild heart attacks
they considered buying a house there, having grown weary of New York City.

Dicht verdichtet das Gedicht,
schützt den Kern vor bösen Sinnen.
Schale, wenn der Kern durchbricht,
weis' der Welt ein dichtes Innen.

Density condenses the poem,
shelters its core from evil intentions.
Shell, when the seed breaks through,
show the world your dense interior.

Arendt is trying to capture poetry in verb form, playing off the word *Dicht* (as in *verdicht, Dichtet,* and *Gedicht*), which means denseness. Poetry, she argued, is dense because it is the form closest to thinking itself. In German, there is a word, *Dichten,* for what it is a poet does. The closest we have in English is *poetize,* but this gives the sense of making something poetic, whereas in German it is poetic in itself and is not made so.

KENTAUR (A PROPOS PLATO'S SEELENLEHRE)

Reite über die Erde
Hin zu den Rändern der Weite
Bis Dein menschlicher Rücken
Sich fügt in die tierischen Schenkel.

Umflügle gebändigt in Dir
Die Erde der Menschen und Rosse,
Denen alles die Herrschaft verdirbt.

Trabend, doch wie im Fluge,
Gestreckt von Gesicht zu den Schenkeln,
Sei ihnen die ältere Einheit
Von Mensch und Tier.

CENTAUR (A PROPOS PLATO'S "DOCTRINE OF THE SOUL")

Ride over the earth
Up to the edges of the world,
Until your human back
fuses with animal thighs.

With tamed wings fly
Over the earth of men and steeds,
For whom mastery ruins everything.

Trot as if in flight
Stretched out from face to flank—
Be for them the ancient union
Of man and animal.

Arendt added "(A propos Plato's Seelenlehre)" to the title in 1953. "Centaur"
is an idiosyncratic reading of Plato's "Doctrine of the Soul" that appears in
Phaedrus. In the dialogue, Plato's Socrates offers the allegory of the charioteer.
The soul, which is immortal and the source of all motion, is described as a
charioteer with a pair of winged steeds. One is a noble creature; the other is sin-
ful and unwilling to yield. Arendt appears to be imagining man—the "noble"
creature—and animal fused together in the mythological figure of the centaur.

Das Alte kommt und gibt Dir nochmals das Geleit.

Kehr nicht das Herz und lass Dich nicht berücken,

Verweile nicht, nimm Abschied von der Zeit

Und wahre Dir den Dank und das Entzücken

Mit abgewandtem Blick.

The past comes and walks by your side once more.
Don't change your heart, don't be charmed.
Don't linger, take leave of the time
And hold on to your gratitude and enchantment
With an averted glance.

It is possible this poem was written for Martin Heidegger's sixty-fourth birthday on September 26, 1953, and enclosed in a letter. In a letter dated October 6, 1953, he writes, "Hannah—Your loving remembrance was a great joy in the hourly and daily path of memory. I am buried in work and still with the Greeks, and it keeps getting more and more illuminating—so it seems to me, at least. I hope you are well. How could it be otherwise—in what endures— Martin." This poem appears in one of her notebooks from 1953, but she did not add it to her poems from 1953 when she collected them.

Ich lieb die Erde
so wie auf der Reise
den fremden Ort,
und anders nicht.
So spinnt das Leben mich
an seinem Faden leise
ins nie gekannte Muster fort.
Bis plötzlich,
wie der Abschied auf der Reise,
die grosse Stille in den Rahmen bricht.

I love the earth,
as if traveling
to a foreign place
and not otherwise.
So life spins me
quietly on its thread
into unknown designs.
Until suddenly,
like a journey's farewell—
the great silence cuts the thread.

Arendt worked and reworked this poem in one of her notebooks. There are three versions, two of which have been fully crossed out.

cuts the thread: In Greek mythology the Fates—Clotho, Lachesis, and Atropos— are divine goddesses who assign individual destinies to mortals at birth. Clotho spins the thread of life, Lachesis measures its allotted length, and Atropos cuts the thread. In *The Odyssey*, Homer writes, "There in the future he must suffer all that Fate and the overbearing Spinners spun out of his life line the very day his mother gave him birth." Since life was predestined for mortal men, what mattered was how they responded to the challenges spun for them by the Fates.

Helle scheint
in jede Tiefe;
Laut ertönt
in jeder Stille.
Weckt das Stumme—
dass es schliefe!—
hellt das Dunkel,
dass uns schuf.

Licht bricht
alle Finsternisse,
Töne singen
jedes Schweigen.
Nur die Ruh'
im Ungewissen
dunkelt still
das letzte Zeigen.

Clarity shines
in every depth;
sound intones
every silence.
Wake up the quiet—
May it sleep!
Illuminate the dark
That created us.

Light breaks
like a note
in the darkness
sounding each silence.
Only the silence
—what we do not know
of darkness—
heralds our final appearance.

Erdennässe
Erdendunst
Süsses irdisches Gewärmtsein
Flockt empor
Zur Wolkenkunst
Sichtbar schwebend im Entferntsein.

Herzenswärme
Herzensgunst
Innig atmendes Gefühltsein
Seufzer leicht
Wie Wolkendunst
Hörbar zitterndes Gerührtsein.

Earth water
Earth air
Sweet earth embodied-being
Steaming up
Into cloud shapes
Visibly hovering in the distant-being.

Heart warmth
Heart grace
Inhaling deep emotional-being
Sighing softly
Like cloud mist
Audibly trembling touched-being.

124

BLUMENFELD ZUM 70TEN GEBURTSTAG

Alles ist schon gesagt
Und nichts bliebt übrig zu singen
Für mich:
Propagandist und Führer
Und Meister der Rede
Architekt des Geistes
Erzieher—Lehrer und Mahner,
Prophet und
   Kammermusikdirigent,
Repräsentant der Epoche,
Konservativer Revolutionär
Und immer unzufrieden,
Kompromise verachtend—
Jähzornig—Freundlich—
   charmant,

Blitzende Augen
Und großer Genießer
Guter Genüsse—
Bruder des Bundes
Und Stürmer und Dränger
Ergründer—Erforscher,
Ewigkeitswerte und
   Gegenwartsarbeit,
Nur der Starke darf
Bündnisse schließen—
Amor Fati und Mutti und
   Großvati—
Und Kinder und Enkel,
Revolution mit langerm Atem,
West-Östlicher Divan und

BLUMENFELD, FOR HIS 70TH BIRTHDAY

Everything has been said
And nothing's left for me
To sing about:
Propagandist and leader
And master of speeches
Architect of minds
Educator—teacher and
    admonisher,
Prophet and chamber music
    maestro,
Representative of an epoch,
Conservative revolutionary
And always unsatisfied,
Scornful of compromise—

Irascible—friendly—*charmant,*
Sparkling eyes
And a great gourmand
Of great pleasures—
Brother of the group
And *Stürmer und Dränger*
Inventor—explorer,
Eternal values and daily work,
Only the strong may
Swear alliances—
Amor Fati and *mutti und großvati*
Children and grandchildren,
A long-lasting revolution,
West-Eastern Divan and

This poem appears in Arendt's correspondence with Kurt Blumenfeld in the German Literature Archive in Marbach. Arendt and Blumenfeld grew close in the years leading up to World War Two, while Blumenfeld was the president of the Zionist Organization of Germany and general secretary for the World Zionist Organization. After the burning of the Reichstag on February 27, 1933, Blumenfeld recruited Arendt to collect antisemitic statements from the Prussian State Library, where she had been conducting research for her book on Rahel Varnhagen. For this work, Arendt was arrested by the Gestapo on charges of "horror propaganda."

This poem is a play on the opening lines of Homer's *Odyssey.*

Stürmer und Dränger: Sturm und Drang, literally translated as "storm and stress," was a proto-Romantic German literary movement that emerged in the latter half of the eighteenth century. It was characterized by its exaltation of nature, individual subjectivity, and extreme emotions. The movement was a rebellion against the Enlightenment's "cult of rationalism."

Amor Fati, the love of fate, refers to an aphorism from Nietzsche in *Ecce Homo.*

West-Eastern Divan: Arendt memorized Goethe's poetry collection *West-Eastern Divan,* inspired by the Persian poet Hafiz.

ewig ein Hatem—
Und Wesenhaft—macher
    jüdischer Werte,
Mit Ranke und Burckhardt
Und Fichtes Rede an die
    Nation—
————
Was bleibt noch zu sagen
Zu stammeln
Dir gegenüber—
Du großer Entwurzler
Und Vergewaltiger Deiner
    Freunde,
Die immer in Angst und
    Bangen
Befürchten den Ausbruch
Vulkanischer Lava—
Immer wenn Gegner und
    Feinde
Sinnlose Dinge erwidern
—Oh Meister und Freund—
Haben doch viele vergessen
Dich als Menschen zu zeichnen
Weil sie distanzvoll
Und immer ein wenig gehemmt
Beter und Anbeter—

Freundliche Priester
Ihrem verehrten Idol
Dankopfer bringen—
Und plötzlich standen wir
    mitten
Auf dem Marktplatz einer
    bekannten Stadt
Wo wir gelernt und gelebt—
Und lernten und machten
    Geschichte—
Und wollten,
Da spät schon die Nacht
Wir uns zu Ruhe begeben,
Dieses Abschiednehmen allein
Ward wieder Roman und
    Romanze,
Denn statt zu enden—
Begannst Du von neuem—
Du ewig neu Beginner—
Wenn andere denken, es geht
    schon zu Ende,
Des Tages Arbeit ist schon
    getan,
Wachtest Du auf mit neuen
    Gedanken,
Und wir hingen am Munde

always a judge—
And intrinsic force behind
   Jewish ethos,
With Rank and Burckhardt
And Fichte's *Address to the
   Nation.*

———

What's left to say?
To stammer
Your way?
You great uprooter
And protector of your friends,
Who always await in fear and
   awe
The explosion
Of your volcanic lava—
Whenever adversaries and foes
Respond with meaningless
   words
—Oh, master and friend—
But many have forgotten
To describe you as a man,
Because they, distanced and a
   bit timid,
Worshipers and supplicants,

Friendly priests,
Bring offerings of thanks
To their honored idol.
And suddenly we stood in the
   middle
Of a marketplace in a well-
   known city—
Where we learned and lived—
And studied and made
   history—
And wanted—
Since the night grew late—
To go get some rest
This farewell itself became
The stuff of novels and
   romances,
Since instead of ending—
You began again—
You eternal new beginner—
When others think it's winding
   down,
The day's work all done,
You were enlivened by new
   thoughts,
And we hung on your mouth's

Address to the Nation: Johann Gottlieb Fichte delivered a series of fourteen weekly lectures that became known as the *Addresses to the German Nation* in 1807 at the Berlin Academy of Sciences to revive the spirit of the people while the city was occupied by Napoleon.

Sokratischer Weisheit
Und beugten uns gern
Überlegener Führung,
Und beschlich uns auch leise
    der Schlaf,
Und wurdest nächtlicher
    Mahner.—
Und wie Du nun saßest—
Freundlich dozierend
Und heiter und launig,
Vor Dir das Bier
Und neben Dir Freunde,
Wie Du sprachst mit weihvoller
    Stimme,
Als ginge es um Großes—

Mit Kellnern—
Über die vielen Gänge
Eines Menus—
Die Bereitung von Saucen und
    Braten,
Und Prüftest vortreffliche
    Weine—
Und dann über Frauen und
    Mädchen—
Natürlich . . .
Bei Shakespeare und Goethe.

————

Das, lieber Kurt, heißt erst
den Menschen menschlich zu
    erfassen.

Socratic wisdom
And gladly deferred
To superior guidance,
And we no longer needed sleep,
You were our nightly
   admonisher.
And the way you sat there—
Affably pontificating
And merry and witty,
A beer before you
And friends beside you,
The way you spoke in solemn
   tones,
As if about something grand—

With waiters—
About the many courses
Of a dinner—
The preparation of sauces and
   sausages,
And taste of excellent wines—
And then about women and
   girls—
Of course . . .
With Shakespeare and Goethe.

———

This, dear Kurt, is the way
To capture a man.

Ein Mädchen und ein Knabe
Am Bach und im Wald,
Erst sind sie jung zusammen,
Dann sind sie zusammen alt.

Draussen liegen die Jahre
Und das was man Leben nennt,
Drinnen wohnt das Zusammen,
Das Leben und Jahre nicht kennt.

A girl and a boy
By a brook in the woods,
First they are young together,
Then they are old together.

Outside the years pass by,
And all that we call life;
But inside dwells togetherness,
Which the years and life can never know.

This poem appears in one of Arendt's notebooks and is framed by a few lines from Bertolt Brecht's *Baal* ("Baal grew up with the whiteness of the womb / With the sky already large and pale and calm") and a fragment from Novalis's *Blütenstaub* ("Die Welt lost sich auf in Figuren und der Zweck in die Handhabung des Universums," or "The world dissolves into figures and purpose in the hands of the universe"). Arendt notes the difference between the living, whose organic nature means they are evolving toward death; the concept of history, which comes from the earth; and the world, which people make. The world, she says, is a vertical line created to run straight through the circular life cycle, gathering layer after layer around itself as it pulls itself up.

GOETHES FARBENLEHRE

Gelb ist der Tag.
Blau ist die Nacht.
Grün liegt die Welt.
Licht und Finsternis vermählen
sich im Dunkeln wie im Hellen.
Farbe lässt das All erscheinen,
Farben scheiden Ding von Ding.

Wenn der Regen und die Sonne
ihrer Wolkenzwiste müde
noch das Trockene und das Nasse
in die Farbenhochzeit einen,
glänzet Dunkles so wie Helles—
Bogenförmig strahlt vom Himmel
Unser Auge, unsere Welt.

GOETHE'S THEORY OF COLORS

The day is yellow.
The night is blue.
The world lies green.
Light and darkness marry
in darkness as in daylight.
Color allows all to appear,
colors separate thing from thing.

When the rain and the sun,
tired of their cloud-quarrels,
unify the dry and wet
in a wedding of colors,
dark will shine like light—
arcing radiant from heaven
our eye, our world.

Published in 1810, Goethe's *Theory of Colors* rejected the long-held belief that color emerges from light, instead arguing that color is shaped by perception and the elements of light and dark *together*. As Goethe wrote, "Color itself is a degree of darkness." *Goethe's Theory of Colours*, Johann Wolfgang von Goethe, trans. Charles Lock Eastlake (London: William Clowers and Sons, 1840), page 31.

Dies Buch grüsst aus der Ferne,
lass es ungelesen *sein*;
Nähe lebt auch in der Ferne,
immer *ist* Gewesensein.

This book greets us from afar,
let it *be* left unread;
For nearness dwells in distance too,
always *is* having been.

SCHWERE SANFTMUT

Sanftmut *ist*
im Inneren unserer Hände,
wenn die Fläche *sich*
zur fremden Form bequemt.

Sanftmut *ist*
im Nacht-gewölbten Himmel,
wenn die Ferne *sich*
der Erde anbequemt.

Sanftmut *ist*
in Deiner Hand und meiner,
wenn die Nähe *jäh*
uns gefangen nimmt.

Schwermut *ist*
In Deinem Blick und meinem,
wenn die Schwere *uns*
ineinander stimmt.

INTENSE TENDERNESS

Tenderness *is*
in the palm of our hands,
when the skin *itself*
befriends foreign forms.

Tenderness *is*
in the arched night sky,
when the distance *itself*
comes to know the earth.

Tenderness *is*
in your hand and mine,
when the nearness *soon*
captures us.

Melancholy *is*
in your gaze and mine,
when the intensity between *us*
draws us into one another.

A more literal translation of the title might be "difficult," or "heavy," softness. Written in one of Arendt's journals, the poem is followed by a note titled "Death," where she writes, "Pain, Rilke: Last Verses—December 1926: 'Come thou, thou last one, whom I recognize, / unbearable pain throughout this body's fabric: / as I in my spirit burned, see, I now burn in thee . . .'" Arendt cites this poem in *The Human Condition* to illustrate how inner pain cannot appear in the world.

So ist mein Herz:
Wie diese rote Scheibe
des Mondes, ganz verhängt von Tränenwolken,
der Nacht bedarf, um glühend
am stillen Brande heiss sich zu verzehren,
auch wie des Holzes heisser Schimmer
im Schwarzen eines nicht mehr leuchtenden Kamins—
So brennt mein Herz in sich und glüht, und leuchtet nicht.

Wenn dann des Tages
mild'res Licht erscheint,
und alle Dinge zeigen sich gestaltet,
und keines hat der Nacht verglühter Brand verzehrt,
—sie kommen heil und schön sich zu gesellen
dem Spiel von Licht und Luft, von Ton und Tau—
so hängt mein Herz dem blassen Sichelmonde gleich
Unscheinbar, unbemerkt und unberührt
am viel zu hellen Himmelsfirmament.

So is my heart:
like this red sliver
of moon, fully covered by clouds
needed by the night to extinguish
its fiery, silent flame,
like the wood's hot shimmer,
no longer molten in the black chimney—
that's how my heart burns and glows, without catching fire.

When the day's more
mild light appears,
and all things reveal their forms,
none consumed by the night's glowing flame,
they accompany safe and sound
the play of light and air, of sound and dew—
then my heart is suspended like a pale crescent moon,
invisible, unnoticed, and untouched
in heaven's far too bright firmament.

Des Glückes Wunde
heisst Stigma, nicht Narbe.
Hiervon gibt Kunde
Nur Dichters Wort.
Gedichtete Sage
ist Stätte, nicht Hort.

The wounds of happiness
are stigmas, not scars.
The only record of this
is the Poet's word.
The poetic saga
is a place, not a refuge.

HOLLAND

Grüne, grüne, grüne Wiesen,
Kühe fleckig auf den Weiden
Himmel hängt die schweren Wolken
tief ins Land hinein.

Braunes, braunes, braunes Wasser
fliesst quadratisch um die Wiesen
in Kanälen: Zaun und Strasse;
stille liegt die Welt.

Menschen knien zwischen Wassern
auf den Wiesen unter Wolken,
hacken nasse, schwarze Erde
weite Welt im Blick.

HOLLAND

Green, green, green pastures,
cows dappled in the meadow,
clouds hang low in the sky
all the way down to the land.

Brown, brown, brown water
flows in angles around the pastures
in canals: fence and street;
silent is the world.

People kneel between waters
in pastures beneath clouds,
tilling wet, black earth,
the wide world in their eyes.

Arendt sent this poem to her husband in a letter from Paris, dated October 9, 1956. She wrote to Blücher that Holland was "in short really like a picture from Ruysdael." Salomon van Ruysdael was a Dutch landscape painter. Arendt appears to be describing his painting "A Country Road" (1648), though he painted several landscapes with cows. In his reply, Blücher wrote, "Darling, The poem is very nice, one has the landscape both in front of one and inside of one."

Schlagend hat einst mein Herz sich den Weg geschlagen
durch fremde wuchernde Welt.

Klagend hat einst mein Schmerz den Wegrand bestellt
gegen das Dickicht der Welt.

Schlägt mir das Herz nun,
so geht es geschlagene Wege,
und ich pflücke am Rain,
was mir das Leben erstellt.

Beating, my heart once beat its way
through a strange and sprawling world.

Plaintively my pain once tended the wayside
against the thicket of the world.

When my heart beats now,
it walks on beaten paths,
and I choose from the fields,
what life has granted me.

Ich seh Dich nur
wie Du am Schreibtisch standest.
Ein Licht fiel voll auf Dein Gesicht.
Das Band der Blicke war so fest gespannt,
als sollt es tragen Dein und mein Gewicht.

Das Band zerriss,
und zwischen uns erstand
ich weiss nicht welches seltsame Geschick,
das man nicht sehen kann, und das im Blick
nicht spricht noch schweigt. Es fand
und sucht ein Lauschen wohl
die Stimme im Gedicht.

I only see you
how you once stood at your desk.
A light falling across your face.
The bond between our eyes was so fixed,
as if it could bear your weight and mine.

The bond broke,
and I don't know what strange fate
arose between us,
no one could see, and in that moment
there was no speaking or silence. It sought
and found a place to be heard:
the voice in the poem.

Ganz vertraut dem Unvertrauten
Nah dem Fremden
Da dem Fernen,
Leg' ich meine Hände in die Deinen.

Wholly familiar, this unfamiliar man,
Almost a stranger,
There so distant,
I place my hand in yours.

Stürzet ein ihr Horizonte,
Lasst das fremde Licht herein;
Ach, die Erde, die Besonnte
Will des Alls gewärtig sein,
Das aus instrumenten Weiten
Sich in Apparaten fängt
Und die irdischen Gezeiten
Donnernd auseinandersprengt.

Collapse, horizons,
Let the strange light in;
Oh, the earth, the sunlit earth
Wants to prepare for the universe
That captures unfathomable
Distances with apparatuses
And thunderously explodes
Earthly tides.

The United States launched its first satellite, Explorer One, into orbit on January 31, 1958.

Der Sturz im Flug gefangen—
Der Stürzende, er fliegt.
Dann öffnen sich die Gründe,
Das Dunkle steigt ans Licht.

The fall caught in flight—
The one who falls, he flies.
Then the ground opens,
The darkness rises to the light.

ERICH NEUMANNS TOD

Was von Dir blieb?
Nicht mehr als eine Hand,
nicht mehr als Deiner Finger bebende Gespanntheit,
wenn sie ergriffen und zum Gruss sich schlossen.

Denn dieser Griff verblieb als Spur
in meiner Hand, die nicht vergass, die
wie Du warst noch spürte, als Dir längst
Dein Mund und Deine Augen sich versagten.

ERICH NEUMANN'S DEATH

What of you remained?
No more than a hand,
no more than the trembling grasp of your fingers,
as they opened and closed in greeting.

For your grasp remained as a trace
in my hand, that never forgot, that
still felt what you were, long after
your eyes and mouth failed you.

Erich Neumann and Arendt were friends during their student days in Hei-
delberg, Germany. According to Elisabeth Young-Bruehl, Neumann sought
Arendt's affections in their youth, but Arendt fell for the expressionist writer
Erwin Loewenson instead. Neumann went on to study with Carl Jung and
became a psychologist.

Dann werd' ich laufen, wie ich einstens lief
Durch Gras und Wald und Feld;
Dann wirst Du stehen, wie Du einmal standst,
Der innigste Gruss von der Welt.

Dann werden die Schritte gezählt sein
Durch die Ferne und Durch die Näh;
Dann wird dieses Leben erzählt sein
Als der Traum von eh und je.

Then I will run as I ran before
Through grass and trees and fields;
Then you will stand as you once stood
The most heartfelt greeting in the world.

Then the steps will be counted
By what is near and what is far;
Then this life will be recounted
as a dream from long ago.

Acknowledgments

When I found Hannah Arendt's poems in the archive at the Library of Congress in 2010 I was still in graduate school working on my dissertation. I made copies and brought them back to Amherst, Massachusetts, where I showed them to my advisor, Thomas Dumm. Tom told me that I should translate them and seeded the idea that they might become a book someday. Tom, thank you for always encouraging me and being a mentor when I needed one most.

Since then, I have carried Arendt's poems with me, working on them over the years in Amherst, Heidelberg, Frankfurt, Paris, Vienna, New York, and Oxford. In this way they have become a part of my inner life, like those poems one memorizes in youth that become part of the mind. For Arendt, I think they were untranslatable, and for me, I will continue to translate them even now that they have appeared in the world. For better or worse.

In 2013, I wrote to Jerome Kohn and formally asked for permission to take on this project. He counseled that Arendt's poems could only be understood through the lens of German poetry, and not just Brecht or Rilke, but Goethe, Hölderlin, and Schiller. I took him at his word, and went to the University of Heidelberg, Arendt's alma mater, to spend two years studying German romantic poetry—the poets Arendt loved most—before I began my work on these translations with a series of grants from the German Academic Exchange Service (DAAD) and the University of Massachusetts Baden-Württemberg Stipendium.

Undertaking this project has been an extremely humbling experience, continuously revealing to me everything I don't know. And having said that, while I have written poems over the course of my life, I have never fancied myself a poet. My translations, while faithful to Arendt's English vocabulary, needed both native German ears and the sensibilities of practiced poets. For my friends in Heidelberg who let me read poems to them for hours on end while asking tedious and prying questions, I am forever indebted. Mark Daniel Letteney spent innumerable hours with me reading through first drafts.

I owe a great debt to Peter Bews, may he rest in peace, who let me take his creative writing classes and workshop informally even after I had left university. He made notes on the first draft of my translations while I was looking for a publisher, and shared sage advice with me over many glasses of sherry. I wish I could give him a copy of this book.

I wish, too, that I could give a copy of this book to Richard Bernstein. May his memory be a blessing. He imparted Arendt's eros to me with his storytelling, and I am forever grateful for the sixteen years of conversations we had, beginning when I was a college senior and journeyed to New York City for the first time alone from Michigan to meet him. I miss his presence in the world dearly.

Several colleagues at Bard College had a hand in reading and editing these poems with me over the years. Ann Lauterbach touched several of these poems. Our conversations helped me think about the more personal aspects of Arendt's verse, and what it meant to bring the private into the public. Thomas Bartscherer read several drafts of this manuscript over the years, offering notes and suggestions, checking passages on Plato and Nietzsche for me, while offering endless support. Thomas Wild offered many insights into Arendt's poetic thinking.

This manuscript would not exist without the incredible work of the archivists who literally guard the storehouse of memory. I am incredibly grateful to Barbara Bair, who oversees Arendt's papers at the Library of Congress, for granting me access to Arendt's poems and sharing enthusiasm for this project. Barbara has gone to the extraordinary measure to open Arendt's archive to the public. And I am forever indebted to Ulrich von Bulow, who granted me access to the German Literature Archive and pulled Arendt's notebooks from a museum display case so I could sit with them. The story about Arendt reciting Schiller is a gift from Ulrich.

Genese Grill brought Arendt's poems to life for me in a fresh way, so that I could see them anew in our editing. Our conversations over translation have brought much joy into my life, Genese measuring meter, me cutting for Arendt's tone. If there's been a third fate among us, it is the dear Rebecca Ariel Porte, who brought us together.

After many years of traveling, I am delighted that Arendt's poems found a home at Liveright. Thank you, Haley Bracken, for your editorial work and patience with this project. And many thanks to my brilliant and generous agent, Kristi Murray, for shepherding this project home.

And I want to thank Suzy, Yono, Sophia, Charlotte, and Maddy for inviting me into their home in Oxford as I finished this book. You have continuously showed me what four walls with love can do, and I love each of you.

I dedicate Hannah Arendt's poems to Jerome Kohn with love and admiration for all he has done to keep Arendt's work alive.

Jerry, this book is for you. Please accept this offering:

The years shall run like rabbits,
For in my arms I hold
The Flower of the Ages,
And the first love of the world.

W. H. Auden, "As I Walked Out One Evening"

Appendix A

Alternate Version and Translation of "Und keine Kunde"

There are two versions of this poem (see page 108 for the other). In the handwritten version that appears in one of Arendt's notebooks there is an additional stanza at the end, which Arendt cut when she typed it up, and some minor variations. The handwritten version of the poem reads:

Und keine Kunde
von jenen Tagen,
die ineinander
sich brennend verzehrten
und uns versehrten:
(des Glückes Wunde
wird Stigma, nicht Narbe).

Davon wär' keine Kunde,
Wenn nicht Dein Sagen
ihm Bleiben gewährte:
(Gedichtetes Wort
ist Stätte, nicht Hort,)

Wenn nicht das Gesichtete
im Leiden Verdichtete,
wenn nicht das Gedenkte

in Lauten Verrenkte
erst dichtend gesprochen,
dann singend gesonnen—
dem Leide entronnen—
ins Bleiben gefügt wär.

And no record
of those tangled
days that were
devoured by flames
and left us burned:
(The wounds of happiness
Become stigmas, not scars.)

There would be no record,
If your account
Had not been imparted—
(Poetic language
is a sanctuary, not salvation).

Were it not for the suffering seen,
transcribed into words,
were it not for thoughts
twisted into sounds
first spoken in poetry,
then sung in song—
escaping from sorrow
into what remains.

Appendix B

Previous Publication History

LC—Library of Congress Archive
YB—Elisabeth Young-Bruehl, *For Love of the World*
AH—Arendt–Heidegger Correspondence
AB—Arendt–Blücher Correspondence
ABC—Arendt–Broch Correspondence
GLA—German Literature Archive

Winter 1923–1924

"No word breaks the dark"—LC, YB, AH.
"In the Tune of a Folksong"—LC, YB, AH.
"Consolation"—LC, YB, AH.
"Dream"—LC, YB, AH.
"Weariness"—LC, YB, AH.
"The Subway"—LC, YB, AH.
"Parting"—LC, YB, AH.

Summer 1924

"Go through days without right"—LC, AH.
"To . . ."—LC, AH.
"This is not happiness"—LC, AH.

"Dusk"—LC, AH.
"Lost in Myself"—LC, YB, AH.

Summer 1925

"Summer Song"—LC, YB, AH.
"Why do you give your hand to me"—LC, YB, AH.
"Goodbye"—LC, AH.
"Late Summer"—LC, YB, AH.

Winter 1925–1926

"October—Late morning"—LC, AH.
"Lament"—LC, AH.
"To the Friends"—LC, YB, AH.
"To the Night"—LC, YB, AH.
"Night Song"—LC, AH.

1942

"W. B."—LC, YB.
"Justice and Freedom"—GLA.

1943

"There are so many memories"—LC, YB.
"Park on the Hudson"—LC, YB.

1946

"Mournfulness is like a flame that has been lit in the heart"—LC, March 1946,
    YB.
"I know that the streets are destroyed"—LC, March 1946.

1947

"Dream"—LC.

"Curse"—LC, July 1947.

"Lord of the nights"—LC, AB July 21, 1947; AB June 1950.

"I am just a little point"—LC, August 1947.

"This was the farewell"—LC, September 1947.

1948

"Dry-drunken, drunken-dry"—ABC, December 30, 1948.

"Incessantly the day distracts us from the One"—LC, September 1948.

1950

"Sometimes the most familiar one comes and opens"—LC, July 1950.

"Rivers without bridges"—1950.

1951

"Oh, who cares"—February 1951. *Denktagebuch*, Vol. 1, Notebook 3, Entry 7, p. 60.

"Distance is only unmeasureable"—LC, YB. *Denktagebuch*, Vol. 1, Notebook 4, Entry 9, pp. 89–90; and Entry 14, pp. 91–92.

"The thoughts come to me"—LC, YB. *Denktagebuch*, Vol. 1, Notebook 4, Entry 13, p. 91.

"H. B."—LC, YB. *Denktagebuch*, Vol. 1, Notebook 4, Entry 15, p. 92.

"Oh, how the"—LC, August 1951. *Denktagebuch*, Vol. 1, Notebook 5, Entry 23, p. 119.

1952

"Only for the one who transforms falling into flight"—LC, March 1952, *Denktagebuch*, Vol. 1, Notebook 8, Entry 20, p. 192.

"Two years in their tides"—March 1952, *Denktagebuch*, Vol. 1, Notebook 8, Entry 24, p. 194.

"Drive through France"—April 1952 / And a second version in the AB correspondence May 1952. / Blücher wrote a variation to Arendt on May 10, 1952; YB, AB. *Denktagebuch*, Vol. 1, Notebook 8, Entry 30, p. 197.

"With one thing"—LC, May 1952. *Denktagebuch*, Vol. 1, Notebook 9, Entry 5, p. 205.

"Endure the abundance"—May 1952, *Denktagebuch*, Vol. 1, Notebook 9, Entry 9, p. 206.

"The end of days"—October 1952, *Denktagebuch*, Vol. 1, Notebook 11, Entry 16, p. 265.

"B's Grave"—LC. A variation of this poem is recorded in *Denktagebuch*, Vol. 1, Notebook 11, Entry 17, p. 265.

"And no record"—December 1952, *Denktagebuch*, Vol. 1, Notebook 12, Entry 25, p. 289.

1953

"Palenville"—LC, August 1953, *Denktagebuch*, Vol. 1, Notebook 17, Entry 27, p. 419.

"Density condenses the poem"—LC. August 1953. *Denktagebuch*, Vol. 1, Notebook 18, Entry 3, p. 424.

"Centaur (A propos Plato's "Doctrine of the Soul")"—LC, September 1953. *Denktagebuch*, Vol. 1, Notebook 18, Entry 21, p. 436.

"The past comes and walks by your side once more"—September 1953, *Denktagebuch*, Vol. 1, Notebook 19, Entry 4, p. 452.

"I love the earth"—LC, November 1953, *Denktagebuch*, Vol. 1, Notebook 19, Entry 29, p. 466.

1954

"Clarity shines"—February 1954, *Denktagebuch*, Vol. 1, Notebook 19, Entry 42, p. 472.

"Earth water"—LC, March 1954, *Denktagebuch*, Vol. 1, Notebook 20, Entry 3, p. 478.

"Blumenfeld, for His 70th Birthday"—GLA.

"A girl and a boy"—August 1954, *Denktagebuch*, Vol. 1, Notebook 20, Entry 30, p. 494.

"Goethe's Theory of Colors"—August 1954, *Denktagebuch*, Vol. 1, Notebook 20, Entry 33, p. 496.

"This book greets us from afar"—October 1954, *Denktagebuch*, Vol. 1, Notebook 20, Entry 41, p. 502.

1955

"Intense Tenderness"—May 1955, *Denktagebuch*, Vol. 1, Notebook 21, Entry 39, pp. 530–31.

1956

"So is my heart"—January 1956, *Denktagebuch*, Vol. 1, Notebook 22, Entry 1, p. 561.

"The wounds of happiness"—January 1956, *Denktagebuch*, Vol. 1, Notebook 22, Entry 17, p. 561–62.

"Holland"—AB, October 9, 1956. *Denktagebuch*, Vol. 1, Notebook 22, Entry 15, p. 567.

"Beating, my heart once beat its way"—November 1956, *Denktagebuch*, Vol. 1, Notebook 22, Entry 17, p. 568.

1957

"I only see you"—*Denktagebuch*, Vol. 1, Notebook 22, Entry 37, p. 584.

1958

"Wholly familiar, this unfamiliar man"—*Denktagebuch*, Vol. 1, Notebook 22, Entry 49, p. 594.

"Collapse, horizons"—August 1958, *Denktagebuch*, Vol. 1, Notebook 23, Entry 17, p. 599.

1959

"The fall caught in flight"—*Denktagebuch*, Vol. 1, Notebook 23, Entry 13, p. 609.

1960

"Erich Neumann's death"—November 30, 1960, *Denktagebuch*, Vol. 2, Note-book 23, Entry 15, p. 613.

1961

"Then I will run as I ran before"—January 1961, *Denktagebuch*, Vol. 1, Note-book 23, Entry 16, pp. 613–14.

Bibliography

Arendt, Hannah. *Denktagebuch: 1950–1973*. Edited by Ursula Ludz and Ingeborg Nordmann. München and Zürich: Piper, 2002.

———. Hannah Arendt Collection. German Literature Archive, Marbach.

———. *The Human Condition*. Chicago: University of Chicago Press, 1998.

———. *Men in Dark Times*. New York: Harcourt, 1968.

———. Papers. Speeches and Writings File, 1923–75, box 85, Poetry and Stories, 1923–25; and box 84, Notebooks Vol. 2, 1942–50. Library of Congress, Washington, DC.

———. *Responsibility and Judgment*. Edited by Jerome Kohn. New York: Schocken Books, 2003.

———. *Thinking Without a Banister: Essays in Understanding, 1953–1975*. Edited by Jerome Kohn. New York: Schocken Books, 2018.

———. "What Remains? Language Remains: A Conversation with Günter Gaus." Transcription of conversation on *Zur Person*, ZDF, October 28, 1964. Translated by Joan Stambaugh, in *Hannah Arendt: Essays in Understanding, 1930–1954*.

Arendt, Hannah, and Heinrich Blücher. *Within Four Walls: The Correspondence Between Hannah Arendt and Heinrich Blücher, 1936–1968*. Edited by Lotte Kohler. New York: Harcourt, 2000.

Arendt, Hannah, and Hermann Broch. *Briefwechsel: 1946 bis 1951*. Edited by Paul Michael Lützeler. Frankfurt am Main: Surkhamp, 1996.

Arendt, Hannah, and Martin Heidegger. *Letters: 1925–1975*. New York: Harcourt, 2004.

Arendt, Hannah, and Karl Jaspers. *Hannah Arendt Karl Jaspers Correspondence, 1926–1969*. Edited by Lotte Kohler and Hans Saner. Translated by Robert and Rita Kimber. New York: Harcourt, 1992.

Arendt, Hannah, and Alfred Kazin. Correspondence. Berg Collection, New York Public Library.

Auden, W. H. "*In Memory of W.B. Yeats.*" In *Another Time*. New York: Random House, 1940.

———. "Thinking What We Are Doing." In *Encounter* 12 (June 1959).

Heidegger, Martin. *Aus der Erfahrung des Denkens*. Pfullingen, Germany: Verlag Günther Neske, 1965.

Jones, Kathleen B. "Hannah Arendt's Female Friends." *Los Angeles Review of Books*, November 12, 2013.

Lowell, Robert. "On Hannah Arendt." *New York Review of Books*, May 13, 1976.

Nietzsche, Friedrich. *The Gay Science: With a Prelude in Rhymes and an Appendix of Songs*. New York: Vintage Books, 1974.

———. *On the Genealogy of Morals and Ecce Homo*. Edited by Walter Kaufmann. New York: Vintage Books, 1969.

———. *Thus Spoke Zarathustra: A Book for All and None*. Cambridge: Cambridge University Press, 2006.

Rilke, Rainer Maria. *Duino Elegies*. Translated by Edward Snow. Berkeley: North Point Press, 2001.

Young-Bruehl, Elisabeth. *Hannah Arendt: For Love of the World*. 2nd edition. New Haven and London: Yale University Press, 2004.

About the Authors

Hannah Arendt (1906–75) was born in Hannover, Germany, into a Jewish-German family. She was forced to flee Nazi Europe in 1941 and made a home in the United States, where she became an influential political thinker. Her books include *The Origins of Totalitarianism*, *The Human Condition*, and *Eichmann in Jerusalem: A Report on the Banality of Evil*.

Samantha Rose Hill is a writer. She is the author of *Critical Lives: Hannah Arendt*, a biography.

Genese Grill is an essayist, a translator, and a scholar of Robert Musil.